TH

CAMEL'S

A Comedy in Three Acts

by

ARNOLD HELSBY

SAMUEL  FRENCH

LONDON

NEW YORK　　TORONTO　　SYDNEY　　HOLLYWOOD

FOR AMATEUR PRODUCTION ENQUIRIES

UNITED KINGDOM AND WORLD EXCLUDING NORTH AMERICA

plays@SamuelFrench-London.co.uk
020 7255 4302/01

Each title is subject to availability from Samuel French, depending upon country of performance.

CHARACTERS.

PRUDENCE HANNACOTT : *A matured spinster, cold, abrupt, domineering.*

TILDA HANNACOTT : *Motherly, emotional and easily swayed.*

FAITH HANNACOTT : *Young, vivacious and altogether lovable.*

ROBERT SLADEN : *A fine upstanding, educated farmer's son.*

NED RUDDLE : *A quaint old stick, terse to the point of rudeness.*

MISS LOVEDAY : *Fussy, quick and bird-like in speech and movement.*

MRS. MIDDLETON-JONES : *The Colonel's wife; very class-conscious.*

SAMUEL MEACOCK : *Big, bluff and hearty.*

CICELY : *The Hannacott help — young, gawky and rather credulous.*

SYNOPSIS OF SCENERY.

ACT I.   *The living-room of the Hannacott Farmhouse.*

TIME: *Saturday morning.*

ACT II.   *The same.* TIME: *Evening, two days later.*

ACT III. *The same.*   TIME: *The following afternoon.*

The Camel's Back

ACT ONE.

*The curtain rises on the living-room of the Hannacott
farm-house.   It is a bright, sunny morning, as
seen through the recessed window in the centre
of the back wall.   There is a door to the right
of the window, opening on to a porch.   There
are doors R. and L. towards the back.   A dresser,
with plate-racks containing the best crockery,
stands to the right of the door in the back wall,
and on the left of the window a warming-pan and
a grandfather clock.   A settee with chintz covers
stands in the window recess.   Towards the front
of the R. wall there are two or three steps
with banister-rails on either side, leading off to
a small landing, where presumably the stairs
take a sudden turn towards the audience.   Over
on the L. wall opposite stands the fireplace.
There is a table, centre, and three chairs; a
rocking-chair by the fire, and a wicker chair
down stage-front on the L.*

*At the opening of the Act, NED RUDDLE is discovered
precariously balanced on a pair of step-ladders,
at the back of the banister-rails.   He is evidently
just finishing hanging a small picture in a
heavy gilt frame over the centre of the stair-
opening, and craning over to give a few final
taps with the hammer.   CICELY, the Hannacott
help, is sitting behind the table finishing her
breakfast.   NED RUDDLE has been so long at the*

5

farm, many years before the late Mr. Hannacott took over, that he has come to be considered as part of the stock and implements. CICELY is young, slightly gawky, and rather credulous.

RUDDLE (*after a final survey*). There! I hope that'll suit you—you old bullfinch!

CICELY. Ned Ruddle! You mustn't be speaking after that fashion. Supposing Miss Hannacott was to hear you?

RUDDLE. Hear me? 'Tis high time she heard somebody in this house—the interfering old buzzard! If I had my way——!

CICELY. There you go again. That's about the twentieth time you've said that!

RUDDLE. Twenty-one. It's three weeks to-day since she came.

CICELY. Well—and what difference have you made with all your brave handsome talk? You've not had your own way—and you're not likely to!

RUDDLE. That's right. You start now! You're like all the rest o' the women in this household. Sticking up for her when she treats you like muck!

CICELY. Fa-ancy tha-at! You know better, you do. I hates the very sight of her.

RUDDLE.—So do Missus—and so does Miss Faith. Yet no sooner does she twiddle her little finger than you're all skipping round her like a circus o' trained fleas!

CICELY. She's a mighty powerful way with her, Ned.

RUDDLE. So has good cheese, when it ain't covered up!

CICELY. Still, I don't see what we're going to do about it. 'Taint for me to speak—I knows my place.

RUDDLE. Meaning as I don't, eh?

CICELY. Well, you're only foreman after all, aren't you?

RUDDLE. I'm not likely to forget that—not while she's around! She orders everybody about as if she owned the blessed place. Why Missus puts up with it I can't see for the life o' me. Why don't she send her packing?

CICELY (*slightly shocked*). Fa-ancy tha-t! Why, dear life—the poor Master'd turn in his grave if he thought his own sister was being turned out. Besides, 'twouldn't be respectful.

RUDDLE. Respectful my foot! She never came here before he went. If she had have done——

CICELY. Yes?

RUDDLE. He'd have gone sooner!

CICELY (*shocked*). Ned Ruddle! Fa-ancy tha-t!

RUDDLE. 'Tis true. Fancy him (*pointing to picture over fireplace*) having a sister like *this*! (*Pointing with hammer at the picture he is hanging.*)

CICELY. Well, the Master had his peculiar little ways.

RUDDLE. Aye, but human—when you knew how to handle him. A thorough-bred he was! (*He sighs.*) And to think this came out o' the same stable! (*Indicating picture.*)

CICELY. Come on down now. You'd better be finishing your breakfast.

RUDDLE. Finishing? I haven't even started! Up since dawn, and just as I comes in and sets me down for a bite, she sails up. "Ruddle," she says—not Ned, mind you; not Ned Ruddle, as was good enough for the Master; nor even Mr. Ruddle! "Ruddle," she says, "I want you to hang my picture!"

CICELY. Fa-ancy tha-at!

RUDDLE. I tried to point out it would do later —that Saturday morning were my busiest time. "At once, Ruddle," she says, "At once, *if* you please!" Then on top o' that she decides she wants it sticking here. Here—of all places! Why it ain't even safe; this panel's as thin as a bit o' matchboard.

CICELY. It's as good a place as any. She couldn't have found a better.

RUDDLE. No, but I could.

CICELY. Where?

RUDDLE. Over the raspberry canes in the garden.

CICELY. Ned Ruddle, you're a horrid old man. Come on and get your breakfast, so I can be clearing off.

RUDDLE. Wait a minute! Come over here, Cicely.

CICELY (crossing). What's the matter?

RUDDLE. Just tell me if this thing's hanging straight, will you? Can't rightly tell from up here.

CICELY. Seems all right to me. My! Ned—she don't look a day above twenty on that photograph. How long ago do you reckon it was since it was taken?

RUDDLE. I dunno. During the Indian Mutiny, probably!

CICELY. Fa-ancy tha-at!

RUDDLE (mocking CICELY and spoken together). Fa-ancy tha-at. Bah!

CICELY. She was quite pretty then, wasn't she?

RUDDLE. Pretty? (Brandishing hammer.) Do you know what I'd like to do to this here picture?

(PRUDENCE enters quietly, L. The other two do not notice her.)

CICELY. What, Ned?

RUDDLE (raising hammer to picture). I'd like to—— !

PRUDENCE (icily). Well?

RUDDLE (tongue-tied). I—I'd like to (meekly) —to hang it a bit higher up.

PRUDENCE. It'll do very well where it is, thank you. (To CICELY.) You, girl!—what are you dawdling about there for? Get those things cleared at once!

CICELY. Yes, Miss Hannacott. But if you please, Ned hasn't finished his breakfast.

RUDDLE. Hasn't started!

PRUDENCE. Then come down and get it. Throwing the whole place out of gear—that's just like a man !

RUDDLE (*descending and expostulating*). But you told me——— !

PRUDENCE. I didn't tell you to be all day about it. Are you quite sure that picture's safe ?

RUDDLE. Aye, it's safe enough—now !

PRUDENCE. Then take those steps away, girl.

(CICELY *complies, taking steps out R.*)

PRUDENCE. And you, Ruddle, hurry up and get your breakfast. I've plenty for you to be doing afterwards. There's been far too much time wasted here in the past, and I'm going to see there's none wasted while I'm here !

RUDDLE (*seated R. of table*). For what we are about to receive———.

PRUDENCE (*sharply*). What's that ?

RUDDLE. I'm saying " Grace."

PRUDENCE. It's quite unnecessary. Time enough for that outside your working-hours. And another thing—I think I've informed you before that I have a name.

RUDDLE (*dipping bread into pot of tea*). Aye, 'tis the usual thing, isn't it ? Though I did hear o' one chap, farm-labourer he was up at Longdeane, has had fifteen children, and he found it more convenient to give 'em a number.

PRUDENCE. An insolent reply, and entirely beside the point ! You know very well what I'm referring to. I'm referring to the fact that in this household I expect to be known as Miss Hannacott.

RUDDLE (*pouring tea into saucer*). Quite right and proper, too. You being the Master's sister. His name was Hannacott—then so be yours. Always providing you ain't secretly married, of course. (*He raises the saucer and drinks.*)

PRUDENCE (*crossing to door L.*). How dare you ! I'll speak to Tilda about this.

RUDDLE (*lifting saucer from mouth*). Tilda ?

PRUDENCE. You know very well who I mean—
Mrs. Hannacott !

RUDDLE. The Missus ?   Oh, aye.   (*Innocently.*)
She's got a name too, hasn't she ?   (*His mouth
returns to the saucer.*)

PRUDENCE. For the last time, will you please
remember if you wish to keep your place here, that
when you speak to me you will address me as *Miss
Hannacott* ! Do you understand ?

RUDDLE. Oh, aye !

PRUDENCE. Aye, what ?

RUDDLE. Aye—I understand.

(*With intense disgust,* PRUDENCE *flounces out through
the door L. Immediately the door over on the
R. opens and* CICELY *re-enters cautiously.*)

CICELY. She's gone, Ned ?

RUDDLE. Aye, she's gone.

CICELY. What was biting her this time ?

RUDDLE. Same old thing. Telling me she's got
a name. Telling *me* !

CICELY. She's got several as I knows of.

RUDDLE. And some as you don't ! At least, if
you do, you're not the girl I imagined you to be.

CICELY. Have you finished now ?

RUDDLE (*pushing plate away*). Just about. That
creature always sets about me when I'm eating.
Spoils my appetite, she does. Reckon she does it
a-purpose.

CICELY. What—to spoil your appetite ?

RUDDLE. No, to save on the groceries !

CICELY (*beginning to clear the table*). Fa-ancy
tha-at ! Things have changed mightily, haven't
they, Ned ? Remember the old days, how we all
used to sit round together at breakfast ? The
Master there, Missus on his right, Miss Faith on the
left, and you and me together opposite.

RUDDLE (*reflectively*). Aye, them were the days !
And look at us now. Meals is more like a wrestling-
match. Catch-as-catch-can ; " Tilda," she says to

the Missus, " Tilda—I can't a-bear to set down at the same table as servants ! " And so we has to sneak in when they're finished, and eat together like a couple of untouchables !

CICELY. Untouchables? What's them?

RUDDLE. Indians as won't allow nobody to touch 'em.

CICELY. My ! They must be awful ticklish. I remember my great-aunt Susan, she couldn't abide——

FAITH (calling off R.). Cicely !

CICELY. Yes, Miss.

FAITH (entering R.). Oh, there you are. Mother wants you in the dairy right away. Don't worry about the table. I'll clear that for you.

CICELY. Very good, Miss. (CICELY exits R.)

FAITH. Hello, Ned. Not finished breakfast yet?

RUDDLE. Practically, Miss.

FAITH. Then why so dismal on such a bright morning? What's the trouble?

RUDDLE. Indigestion.

FAITH. Indigestion? (Moving to dresser.) Then you'll have to have a dose of bi-carbonate.

RUDDLE. No, Miss—not that kind. Nothing to do with the stomach. Mental Indigestion.

FAITH (returning). Mental Indigestion? Where did you get that from?

RUDDLE (pointing to picture above stairs). There !

FAITH (coming down to examine picture). What, this picture?

RUDDLE. Aye, that's a sample of what it was like in its early stages.

FAITH. I can't make it out properly. Who is it?

RUDDLE. Your Aunt.

FAITH. Aunt Prudence? (Laughing.) Good heavens! It's not a bit like what she is now.

RUDDLE. Oh, it's her all right. " Never mind your breakfast," she says, " get my picture hung." Brought it all the way from Barncastle, she has;

carried it herself so as to be sure as it wouldn't get damaged.

FAITH. Well, I suppose that's her idea of brightening the place up a bit.

RUDDLE (*rising and going over L.*). Brightening the place up? That there picture's a warning, it is, —a solemn warning!

FAITH. What do you mean, Ned?

RUDDLE. What does a chap do who marries a widow with a pub? The first thing he does is to get his name over the door. Same with her. She's nailing her colours to the mast. She's here to stop!

FAITH (*with a sigh*). Yes, I'm afraid she is.

RUDDLE. But for why? Why put up wi' it? That's what I can't understand.

FAITH. That's exactly it. You don't understand.

RUDDLE. Listen, Miss Faith. Pardon a bit o' plain speaking, but I reckon we've always been pretty good friends, eh?

FAITH. The best, Ned.

RUDDLE. Then you'll forgive me asking a personal question or two?

FAITH (*sitting on front edge of table*). Of course, you old silly!

RUDDLE. Right, then here goes. First—you don't like her yourself, do you?

FAITH. No, Ned, I don't.

RUDDLE. There—I needn't have asked that! 'Twas evident from the way you've been moping about these last three weeks.

FAITH. Good gracious! I hope I haven't looked as big a misery as that.

RUDDLE (*patting her hand and sitting on chair L. of table*). You couldn't be a misery if you tried, Miss. What I means is, when you've been on your own in a quiet corner, or when—(*pointing to picture*)—the Death of Nelson's been around.

FAITH. I see. Well, that's one question answered. What about the others?

RUDDLE. Second.   The Missus don't like her either ?

FAITH. Mother ?   No, I don't believe she does.

RUDDLE. Then why in the name o' thunder don't somebody do something about it ?   Why don't you up and tell her to pack her bags, and leave the running o' this farm to them as knows something about it ?

FAITH. It can't be done.   In any case, it isn't my place to interfere.   Mother's in charge here.

RUDDLE. Then why don't the Missus tell her ?

FAITH. Because she can't.

RUDDLE (*rising*). Afraid of her, eh ?   I'm blessed if I can see why !

FAITH (*also rising*). Listen, Ned. I'm going to tell you something you ought to have been told before.   It's really a secret—but as you've been here longer than anybody, I don't see why you shouldn't know.   She *is* here to stay !

RUDDLE. I knew it !   Must have been something to do with the will, eh ?

FAITH (*sitting once more on table edge*). Exactly. You see it was this way.   When Father died, he was terribly worried about the future of this place. He felt that it was too great a responsibility for Mother, because she never had much of a head for business or figures.

RUDDLE. No, baking was always her line.

FAITH. In the same way, Father considered that I was too young and inexperienced for the job of managing a farm like this.

RUDDLE. I'm beginning to get at it now.   So he looked round for somebody as he thought could ?

FAITH. And picked on his sister, Aunt Prudence. He hadn't seen much of her for a long time.   All he knew about her was that she'd had a draper's shop over in Barncastle, and that she'd retired from it with enough money to keep her comfortably for the rest of her days.

RUDDLE (*sitting L. of table*). There ain't enough money minted to keep her—comfortably !

FAITH. And so you see—she'd made a success of one business, so Father must have thought she could make a success of another.

RUDDLE. Aye, but farming ain't selling drapery. She'd be better measuring cows for petticoats than trying to milk 'em ! Howsomever, what was said about it in the will ?

FAITH. Father expressed a wish that as his sister lived on her own, she should come and make her home here, and help Mother and I to manage the farm.

RUDDLE. Christopher Columbus ! Then she's here *for good* ?

FAITH. Not quite ! Father said that she was to stay here if she wished, until I was twenty-five.

RUDDLE. Twenty-five ? And how old are you now ?

FAITH (*smiling*). Really, Ned. That's hardly the question to ask a lady, surely ?

RUDDLE. Begging your pardon, Miss Faith, but in this here case it's mighty important that I should know the truth. The condemned man has every right to hear sentence passed afore they takes him away.

FAITH. Well, if it will help you to reckon—I was nineteen last birthday.

RUDDLE (*stunned, rising and going L.*). Six years ! Six years' hard labour ! (*Bitterly.*) And no remission for good conduct.

FAITH. There may be a remission, though.

RUDDLE (*eagerly*). What do you mean, Miss ?

FAITH. The will said she could stay here until I was twenty-five, or alternatively, until I got married.

RUDDLE (*coming back centre*). Reprieved! Merciful heavens! Reprieved on the very scaffold!

FAITH. What do you mean ?

RUDDLE. Why, we've got to get you married as soon as possible. The sooner—the better !

FAITH (*rising*). Wait a minute, though, Ned. There's still something else.

RUDDLE. Something else ? In the will ?

FAITH. Yes. You see, I may not marry before I am twenty-five, without the full consent and approval of my Aunt.

RUDDLE. But that's monstrous—inhuman ! 'Tis your Mother should decide that.

FAITH. Exactly ; but Father thought not.

RUDDLE (*going away a little to the L.*). The Master must have gone crazy, he must !

FAITH. So you see, if you're going to get me married, you'd better pick someone Aunt Prudence approves of—or else—(*She turns her thumbs down.*)

RUDDLE. That ain't going to stop us ! I'll have every chap in the village propose to you. We'll either find one as suits her, or wear her down.

FAITH. Wait a minute, Ned. What about suiting me ?

RUDDLE (*up to* FAITH). Aye, to be sure. Forgive me , Miss, I was thinking more o' the six years than you. (*Slyly.*)   Still, I don't think either of you would jib so much, if the young fellow you chose to hitch up to were something like—like young Bob Sladen, shall we say ?

FAITH. I mightn't—but you know what she is.

RUDDLE. Rubbish ! Bob's forgotten more about farming than she'll ever know. You have a packet at it, Miss, and if you manage to get her away from here——

FAITH. Well ?

RUDDLE. I'll stand godfather to the first three !

FAITH (*laughing*). Get away with you, Ned ! I never heard such talk.

TILDA (*off*). Ned Ruddle !

FAITH. Look out ! Here's Mother. (*Going back R.*) Not a word about this. You're not supposed to know. remember.

RUDDLE (*remaining C.*). Trust me, Miss. I'll be as silent as the grave.

TILDA (*entering R.*).   Oh, here you are, Ned ! Have you finished your breakfast ?

RUDDLE. Yes, Missus.

TILDA. Then you might come and attend to this man from the Railway Company.

RUDDLE. What's he want ?

TILDA. It's to do with the milk-cans.   Some of them got lost or stolen or something. You'll find him out there by the shippens.

RUDDLE. Very good, Missus. I'll see to it. (*He crosses to the door at the back. As he does so, he slips his hand in his pocket and produces a couple of pot eggs. He looks at them, and then crosses to TILDA, handing them to her.*)

RUDDLE. While I remember, Missus ; you might give these back to Miss Hannacott.

TILDA. What on earth ? Pot eggs ! What does she want with these ?

RUDDLE. She'd put 'em in one o' the pens out-side. Said she'd make the birds jealous—incite 'em to lay a bit more.

TILDA.   Well, there's nothing wrong in that, surely ?

RUDDLE (*back at the door*). Nothing much. Only that pen's full o' young cockerels !

(*He exits via the back door. FAITH laughs, TILDA looks puzzled.*)

TILDA. Faith, I don't think Ned Ruddle's very fond of your Aunt.

FAITH. No more than the rest of us, Mother.

TILDA (*ignoring this last remark*). And she's just as much against him. She's tried to persuade me at least three times this week to get rid of him.

FAITH. Get rid of Ned ! Oh, but surely, Mother, you'd never do a thing like that ? Ned's the main-stay of this place. You could never replace *him*.

TILDA. I know, dear. But your Aunt's a very

powerful woman. She gets her way in most things in the long run.

FAITH (*sitting L. of table*). Then it's high time we put a stop to it !

TILDA. What do you mean, dear ?

FAITH. I mean it's high time you put your foot down. You've got to let her see that you're the boss here—and the sooner the better !

TILDA (*glancing nervously around*). That's all very well, but——

FAITH (*angrily*). She's a horrid old tyrant, that's what she is !

TILDA (*very concerned*). Hush, Faith dear ! You mustn't say things like that. She might hear you.

FAITH. And so she shall. You're afraid of her, Mother, that's what it is—downright afraid ! And if you won't assert yourself and turn her out—then I shall !

TILDA. But how do you think you're going to do that ?

FAITH. By getting married.

TILDA (*astounded*). WHAT !

FAITH. By getting married.

TILDA (*collapsing into chair R. of table and dabbing handkerchief to her eyes.*) Oh, Faith ! And you never told me anything about it !

FAITH. Of course not, Mother. I never thought of it seriously till just now.

TILDA. And who is the—the lucky young man ?

FAITH. Bob Sladen.

TILDA. Bob Sladen ? Ah, well, I've nothing to say against him. A decent lad, by all reports. But I do at least think he might have asked me first.

FAITH. Give him a chance, Mother. He hasn't asked *me* yet.

TILDA (*more astounded*). WHAT !

FAITH (*laughing and crossing over behind* TILDA's *chair*). That's all right, Mother. He *will* do—I can tell.

TILDA. How?

FAITH. By the look in his eyes. I'm sure it's been on the tip of his tongue many a time just lately.

TILDA. You don't want to take any notice of the way they look. When your Father asked me he looked as though he was having a tooth out!

FAITH. Yes, but how did he look afterwards— when you'd said " Yes "?

TILDA. Resigned. Very resigned !

FAITH (*laughing and hugging* TILDA). Oh, Mother, you're hopeless.

TILDA (*rising*). Well, I wish you luck, dear. But even if he does ask you, what will your Aunt have to say about it?

FAITH (*going over L. to fireplace*). That's what I'm going to find out—*now* !

TILDA. What ! Before he's asked you?

FAITH. Yes, then I shall know how the land lies.

TILDA. But, Faith—— !

(*The door on the L. opens, and* PRUDENCE *enters.*)

PRUDENCE. Good gracious me ! Isn't this table cleared yet? Where's that girl got to?

FAITH (*clearing remaining things*). It's all right, Aunt Prudence. I'll attend to it. Cicely's busy in the dairy.

PRUDENCE. Then she'd no right to leave it unfinished ! One job at a time, that's my motto. Well, Tilda, nothing to do this morning? (*Crossing to* TILDA.)

TILDA. Yes, Prudence, I was just going to——

PRUDENCE. That's right ! No time to waste in a busy place like this. Where's Ruddle?

TILDA. Out in the yard talking to the man from the Railway Company.

PRUDENCE. Well, I want to see him. I've got an idea.

TILDA. An idea?

PRUDENCE. Yes, for getting more milk. (*Proudly.*) And do you know how I'm going to do it?

FAITH (*brightly, as she passes back to dresser*). Yes. Buy some more cows!

PRUDENCE (*snappishly*). Of course not, child! (*Going L.*) Maybe you think that's very clever. Modern education has a lot to answer for, Tilda, if this is a sample of what the schools are turning out nowadays.

TILDA (*busying herself at the dresser*). Yes, I suppose you're right.

PRUDENCE. Of course I'm right. I'm always right! If I hadn't been, I should never have raised myself to my present position. Faith, you'd better run along to the dairy and let that girl get back to the kitchen. I'll see that Ruddle isn't wasting his time! (*She moves to the back door.*)

FAITH. Just a minute, Aunt. I'd like to speak to you.

PRUDENCE (*turning*). Well, what it is? Be sharp, I've no time to spare. (*She sits L. of table.*)

FAITH. I—I've been thinking of getting married!

PRUDENCE (*hardening*). You've what?

FAITH. I've been thinking of getting married!

PRUDENCE. Then forget it! Now you run along and send that girl——

FAITH. Listen, Aunt. This is serious.

PRUDENCE. You foolish child! Do you mean to tell me that you—*you*—are seriously contemplating matrimony? Why, you're little more than a baby!

FAITH. I'm nineteen!

PRUDENCE. Indeed, quite a matured spinster in your own estimation, I suppose? And who's the man who's fool enough to want to marry you?

FAITH. I haven't quite decided yet. (*Sitting R. of table opposite* PRUDENCE.)

PRUDENCE. What on earth! Is the girl mad?

FAITH. No, you see, quite a number have asked me.

PRUDENCE. What—proposed to you?

FAITH. Yes. Only before I accept any one of them, I thought I'd find out what kind of a man you approve of, then I should know which one to pick.

PRUDENCE. So? You want to know what kind of a young man I approve of?

FAITH. Yes, if you don't mind, Aunt.

PRUDENCE. Then I'll tell you. None!

FAITH. None? But surely——?

PRUDENCE. Listen, child. You're far too young to think about marriage. Later on—maybe, yes. When you're twenty-five there'll be time to think about such things.

FAITH (*rising*). I see. So you would never consent to my marrying anyone until after I'm twenty-five?

PRUDENCE (*also rising*). Absolutely! Not under any conditions whatsoever.

FAITH. And supposing I marry without your approval?

PRUDENCE. I think the terms laid down in your Father's will made that quite clear. Your Mother and I would be able to carry on quite well without you!

TILDA (*coming up from dresser*). Oh, Faith!

FAITH (*going to* TILDA). Don't worry, Mother. I'd never leave you in the lurch like that.

PRUDENCE. Come, Tilda! We will now consider this matter closed. You, Faith, had better be looking to the dinner. We'll relieve Cicely in the dairy. Come along, Tilda!

(TILDA *and* PRUDENCE *exit through the door* R. FAITH *wanders disconsolately towards the window.* ROBERT SLADEN *suddenly crosses past the window. He waves to* FAITH *and she waves back. She runs to the back door, opens it and* BOB *enters. He keeps his hands behind his back.*)

FAITH. Bob Sladen! What are you doing here this time of day? Has something gone wrong over at Applegarth Farm?

BOB. Not a bit of it, Faith.   Got some news, that's all.   Was over to the station about a consignment of pigs, when I ran into Miss Loveday.

FAITH. The schoolmistress !   What's she to do with it ?

BOB. A lot !   You can't guess what I've got.

FAITH (*excitedly*). I know.   The parts for the Dramatic !

BOB (*producing them from behind his back*). Right first time !   There's yours.

(FAITH *seizes it and begins to turn the pages rapidly. She comes to front of table and sits at R. end of it.*)

BOB (*coming down L. of table*). Miss Loveday gave me my book.   Then when she said she was coming over here with some other parts, I begged yours of her and ran on ahead so that you'd know about it before the others.

FAITH. " Love and the Locksmith."   What a grand title !

BOB. Isn't it ?

FAITH. And what part do I play ?

BOB (*pointing*). The heroine—Patricia.

FAITH. And you ?

BOB (*proudly*). The hero—James !

FAITH. Oh, how lovely !   What do *we* have to do ?

BOB. Let's try a bit of it, shall we ?   We shall have to hurry up, though.   Miss Loveday'll be here in a few minutes.

FAITH (*rising*). Why didn't you bring the other books along with you, then you would have saved her the journey ?

BOB. Because she said she wanted to see your Mother particularly. To ask a favour or something.

FAITH. I see.

BOB. Well, what about it ?   Are we going to read a bit of it now ?

FAITH. Yes, Bob, if you like. Where shall we begin?

BOB. What about page nineteen—half-way down.

FAITH. Wait a minute—Yes, I've got it! Who starts?

BOB. You do—there, see (*Pointing to her book.*)

FAITH (*reading*). "James, you must go now. If my Father were to find you here, there would be a terrible scene."

BOB (*reading*). "Patricia, I'm not afraid. I'd dare far worse things than that—to be with you!"

(*He slips his arm around her.*)

FAITH. Bob Sladen! That's not in the book!

BOB. No, but it's going to be in the part! Carry on!

FAITH. "If only I could be sure of you, sure that you really cared."

BOB. "Cared?" — (*Presumably reading aloud stage-direction*)—"Taking her in his arms——"

(*Business of trying to take her in his arms. Eventually they succeed. BOB holding his book in one hand, the audience side, FAITH vice-versa.*)

BOB. "Cared? Patricia—I love you!"

FAITH (*looking up from book into his eyes*). "Do you really mean that, Bo—, —(*looking down sharply and correcting herself*)—James?"

BOB. "Mean it? Ever since I first came to this house, sleeping, waking, the only thing in my thoughts has been the vision of you. I love you, Faith!"

FAITH (*correcting him*). Patricia!

BOB (*glancing back at his book*). Patricia.

FAITH. "And I love you too!"

BOB (*reading stage-direction*)—"They kiss"—

(*FAITH looks up. BOB hesitates for a moment, then draws her slowly towards him. He kisses her, and his book falls to the ground behind her back.*)

BOB (*still holding her*). Then I only want your answer—tell me—Will you marry me ?

FAITH (*endeavouring to look at her book*). Bob Sladen. That's not in the book !

BOB. The book doesn't matter, dear. Nothing matters now. Faith—will you marry me ?

FAITH. Oh, Bob !

BOB. Come on, dear, what's it to be ?

FAITH. Yes, Bob, if you want me.

BOB. Faith !

(*They kiss again. FAITH's book also tumbles to the ground. The door at the back opens suddenly, and NED RUDDLE appears. As soon as he sees the pair embracing, he raises arm and gives a loud " Hurrah ! "*)

FAITH (*separating and picking up books*). Oh—er—it's you, Ned ! We were just rehearsing a play, that's all.

RUDDLE. Aye—I remember saying the same thing myself once. But it made no difference.

FAITH. Why, Ned ?

RUDDLE. Her father kicked me out—just the same !

BOB. Ned Ruddle, I want you to congratulate me. I'm the happiest man in the world. Faith has just consented to become my wife.

RUDDLE. Congratulate you, Bob Sladen ?—that I will ! (*He shakes BOB warmly by the hand.*)

BOB. You don't know what this means to me.

RUDDLE (*still pumping his arm vigorously*). No, and you don't know what it means to us !

FAITH (*suddenly realising*). Oh, Bob, I'd forgotten—I'm afraid I can't marry you after all !

BOB (*astounded*). Can't what ?

FAITH. I can't marry you—at least, not for a long, long time.

BOB. What on earth——?

RUDDLE. It's all right, Bob. It takes 'em like this sometimes. When you've seen as much o' women as I have——

FAITH. No, Ned, it's true! You see, Bob, according to my Father's will, I can only marry before I'm twenty-five with the full consent and approval of Aunt Prudence.

BOB. Well, we'll soon get that!

FAITH. I'm afraid not. You see, I tackled her about it only a few minutes ago, and she flatly refused.

BOB. But she can't have anything against me?

FAITH. It isn't you; she's against anything that might prevent her ruling this household with a rod of iron for the next six years.

BOB. The old scarecrow!

RUDDLE (*feelingly*). I can find you some better ones than that!

BOB. Then we'll marry without her consent. There'll always be a home waiting for you over at Applegarth, Faith.

FAITH. What—leave poor Mother to suffer under her alone?

RUDDLE (*very feelingly*). And me, Miss! *And me!* (*Going back.*)

FAITH. No, Bob. There must be some other way out, and we've got to find it.

BOB. Yes—but how——?

RUDDLE (*turning*). Wait a minute! Was anything said in the will about if she got fed up here and went away herself?

FAITH. Yes. If ever she leaves here of her own accord, then I shall be free to do as I please.

RUDDLE (*coming down*). Then the whole thing's settled! All we've got to do is to make her depart of her own sweet will—and then everything in the garden's lovely!

BOB. Yes, but how——?

RUDDLE. There must be hundreds of ways. You leave this to me. If I don't get her out of here, and before long too, then my name's not what it is !

BOB. Ned Ruddle—on the day she leaves this house for good—it'll be worth a pound note in your pocket.

RUDDLE. Done ! (*He shakes hands with* BOB.) Look out ! There's somebody coming !

(MISS LOVEDAY *and* MRS. MIDDLETON-JONES *pass across behind the window.* FAITH *crosses to the door at the back and opens it to greet the visitors.*)

LOVEDAY (*entering*). Good-morning, Faith, my dear. You got your part, I suppose ? **Ah** yes, there's Mr. Sladen. Ah, you naughty man—depriving me of my big surprise ! And Mr. Ruddle, too ! Well, well ! It isn't often we have the opportunity of meeting you. And how is Mr. Ruddle, may I ask ?

RUDDLE. Passable, ma'am, thank-ee. Very passable.

LOVEDAY. I met the dear Colonel's wife on the way, so I took the liberty of bringing her along with me.

FAITH. You're welcome, Mrs. Middleton-Jones.

MIDDLETON-JONES. Thank you, my dear. Good-morning, gentlemen !

BOB }
RUDDLE } (*together*). {Good-morning, Ma'am.
{ Mornin', Ma'am.

FAITH. Were you wanting to see Mother ?

LOVEDAY. Yes, my dear, we did rather. And your Aunt, too—(*turning to* MRS. MIDDLETON-JONES) —I think ?

MIDDLETON-JONES. Yes, the Aunt too, most decidedly—the Aunt too.

FAITH. Then I'll run and find them—they're down in the dairy, I believe.

(*The door R. opens.*)

Oh, they're here now.

(TILDA *enters, followed by* PRUDENCE.)

LOVEDAY. Ah, there you are, dear Mrs. Hannacott ! Faith was just going to find you.

TILDA. Miss Loveday !—and Mrs. Middleton-
Jones too ! This is a pleasure. It isn't often we
get you both down here together.

MIDDLETON-JONES. How do you do, Mrs. Hannacott ?

TILDA. Let me see—you haven't met my sister-
in-law, Miss Hannacott. This is Miss Loveday, the
schoolmistress.

LOVEDAY }
PRUDENCE } (*together*). How do you do !

TILDA. You know the Colonel's wife, of course ?

MIDDLETON-JONES. Dear Miss Hannacott and I
had quite a delightful little chat after the service
last Sunday.

PRUDENCE. Ruddle ! You may go now.

MIDDLETON-JONES. No, please—we'd like Mr.
Ruddle to stay, if you don't mind, dear ?

PRUDENCE. Very well. Won't you sit down ?

LOVEDAY. Thank you. (*They sit;* PRUDENCE R. *of
table,* LOVEDAY C. *and* MIDDLETON-JONES L.) Well,
Mrs. Hannacott, as you may no doubt have guessed
by now, I've called about the parts.

PRUDENCE. The parts ?

TILDA (*standing R. by* PRUDENCE). Miss Loveday
is the producer of our Village Dramatic Society.

LOVEDAY. Yes, Miss Hannacott, we're producing
three One-Act Plays shortly in the schoolroom.

MIDDLETON-JONES. In aid of the Church Funds.

LOVEDAY. Miss Faith and Mr. Sladen here have
both kindly consented to play parts as usual, and
we were wondering if you, Mrs. Hannacott, would

be so kind as to help us out by playing a small part in one of the plays?

TILDA. Well—really—I'd like to, Miss Loveday, but I'm afraid I was such a failure in the last.

MIDDLETON-JONES. Nonsense, dear Mrs. Hannacott! You prompted excellently. I could hear you quite distinctly myself from the back of the hall.

LOVEDAY. Yes, you will promise to help us, won't you? I wouldn't have troubled you if we hadn't been absolutely stuck—er, I mean if we hadn't considered you the only person in the village to fit the part.

TILDA. Very well, I'll try, if you insist. But I'm afraid I shall be the worst person on the stage.

LOVEDAY. Not you, dear. (*Unthinkingly.*) The dear Colonel's wife is playing as well, you know!

(MRS. MIDDLETON-JONES *draws herself up stiffly, but* MISS LOVEDAY *prattles on gaily, quite unconscious of the "faux pas."*)

LOVEDAY. And what about you, Miss Hannacott?

PRUDENCE. I?

LOVEDAY. Yes, we were hoping to persuade you to take a part in one of the plays.

PRUDENCE. Ridiculous! Why, I've never done anything of the sort in my life.

MIDDLETON-JONES. Come, come, now, Miss Hannacott. You under-estimate your abilities. I can picture you as a perfect—now what was the name of that charming lady in one of Shakespeare's plays?

RUDDLE (*over L. with* BOB—*helpfully*). Lady Macbeth?

MIDDLETON-JONES. No, no, that wasn't the one! Ah well, it doesn't matter. But you will help us, won't you, dear Miss Hannacott?

PRUDENCE. Well—I——

LOVEDAY (*rising*). There! I knew you wouldn't refuse us. Here's the book, Miss Hannacott. "Love and the Locksmith," and I want you to take the part of the Mother.

(BOB *and* FAITH *exchange significant glances.*)

And here's your book, Mrs. Hannacott. Yours is the second play: "Age Shall Not Wither," and I want you to take the part of Miss Berryman.

TILDA. I'll do my best, Miss Loveday, though I don't feel too happy about it.

LOVEDAY. Don't worry. You'll be all right. You have your copy, Faith?

FAITH (*back-stage R.*). Yes, thank you.

LOVEDAY. And you, Mr. Sladen? Ah yes, of course, I gave it to you, didn't I? Silly of me! (*She simpers.*)

MIDDLETON-JONES. Miss Loveday! You haven't forgotten about Mr. Ruddle?

RUDDLE (*startled*). Eh?

LOVEDAY (*sitting again behind table*). Ah yes, of course. As you are well aware, Mrs. Hannacott, there is an acute shortage of men in the Society, and in view of our ambitious programme, we were wondering if you would give permission for Mr. Ruddle to take a very small part?

TILDA. It's all right as far as I'm concerned. What do you say, Ned?

RUDDLE. Not likely!

PRUDENCE. Ruddle! You forget yourself! Yes, Miss Loveday, he'll take the part.

LOVEDAY (*rising*). I'm so glad. I knew you would, Mr. Ruddle. There's the book—the butler in "Love and the Locksmith"—it's only a few lines.

RUDDLE. Couldn't you make it a maid, ma'am, and give it to Cicely? She's always wanted to go on the films.

LOVEDAY. No, I'm afraid we couldn't. You'll manage all right.

MIDDLETON-JONES. Miss Loveday — you haven't forgotten about rehearsals?

LOVEDAY (*sitting*). Ah yes, of course. I've still another favour to ask of you, dear Mrs. Hannacott. As you know, with three plays it's going to be rather difficult about rehearsals; especially as the schoolroom is taken up so much in the evenings with Mothers' Union, the Scouts and what-not. So we've been wondering if you would let us rehearse one of the plays here? " Love and the Locksmith " perhaps—seeing that so many of you are in it?

TILDA. I don't see why not—(*nervously*)—that is unless you have any objection, Prudence?

PRUDENCE. None.

LOVEDAY. Then we'll consider that settled. Let me see—to-day is Saturday. Then we'll hold the first rehearsal here on Monday evening. Monday, at eight o'clock! Is that agreed?

OMNES. Yes.

LOVEDAY. Good! I hope you won't mind coming along here to rehearse, Mr. Sladen?

BOB (*with a glance at* FAITH). I shall be delighted.

LOVEDAY (*standing once more*). Very well, then. All of you try to get off as much of your parts as possible before Monday. (*Turning to* MRS. MIDDLE-TON-JONES.) And now we must really be going.

TILDA. You'll stay and have a cup of tea, surely?

LOVEDAY (*returning to seat*). Well, for myself, I wouldn't mind—What about the dear Colonel's wife?

MIDDLETON-JONES. I've several calls to make yet. Still, just one cup perhaps.

PRUDENCE (*opening door R.*). Cicely! (*Returning to the others.*) We'll have it served out in the garden. It's such a beautiful morning—shame to be indoors.

CICELY (*entering*). You called me, Miss Hannacott?

PRUDENCE. Yes, child. How long will it take you to make some tea?

CICELY. Only a minute or so, ma'am. The kettle's boiling now.

PRUDENCE. Good ! Then serve it out in the garden.

CICELY. Yes, ma'am.

PRUDENCE. And another thing. I want you to open the canister on the top shelf—the one I brought with me from Barncastle.

CICELY. Yes'm. (*She goes.*)

PRUDENCE. It's very special tea. Comes from a cousin of mine who's out in Ceylon. He says it's a new blend. I haven't tried it myself yet.

MIDDLETON-JONES. Oh, how lovely ! I'm quite looking forward to it.

PRUDENCE. Then shall we go out into the garden? Come along, Miss Loveday. I'd like to show you my standard-roses. I've got a new idea for——

(PRUDENCE, MISS LOVEDAY, TILDA *and* MRS. MIDDLE-TON-JONES *exit through the back door, chattering noisily. They make over to the R., and do not pass the window.*)

BOB. I say, that's going to be great, isn't it ?

RUDDLE. What—me as a butler? Bah !

BOB. No, I mean rehearsing here.

FAITH (*up R.*). Yes, but that doesn't solve our problem, does it ?

BOB (*a little dashed*). Oh—I'd forgotten about that.

RUDDLE (*slapping his knee*). Got it !

BOB. What's up ?

RUDDLE (*crossing L.*). Bob Sladen, you don't happen to have that pound note about you, I suppose ?

BOB (*feeling in his pocket*). Yes, I reckon so. Why ?

RUDDLE. Then hand it over. I'm going to earn it.

BOB (*holding note*). Yes, but look here——

RUDDLE (*taking note*). That's all right. Just wait a moment. I'll show you. (*He crosses to the door R. and calls.*) Cicely !

CICELY (*entering*).   Yes, Ned Ruddle ?   What is it ?   I'm busy.

RUDDLE.   Is that tea ready.

CICELY.   Almost brewed.   I'm just waiting to pour it.   Why ?

RUDDLE (*bringing her C. behind table*).   Come here, Cicely.   You'd like to earn half-a-crown, I reckon ?

CICELY.   Oh yes, Ned !

RUDDLE.   Then listen to me.   (*He produces a glass flask from his pocket containing a colourless liquid.*)   You see this flask.   All you've got to do is put a good dose o' this in Miss Hannacott's tea-cup —Miss Hannacott's mind you—and the half-crown's yours.

CICELY.   Oh, Ned, you ain't going to poison her ?

RUDDLE.   Nothing of the sort !   This stuff's perfectly harmless.   Now you run along, and so soon as you can assure me Miss Hannacott's had some o' that, the money's yours.

CICELY.   All right.   I'll do it, Ned.   But if she dies——

RUDDLE (*pushing her off R.*)   Get along with you.   She won't die.   She won't even know she's had it, I promise you.

(CICELY *exits through the door R.*)

BOB.   Look here, Ned Ruddle.   What's the idea ?

RUDDLE.   What's the idea ?   You want the old buzzard shifted out o' here. don't you ?   Well, I'm going to do it, that's all.

BOB.   But, good heavens, man !   You can't go putting drugs or something in her tea !

FAITH.   Why, it's a criminal offence, isn't it ?   You'll land us all up in the police-court !

RUDDLE.   Drugs, my foot !   I'm not after kidnapping her or anything like that.   Not likely !

FAITH.   Then what are you trying to do ?

RUDDLE.   Shame her !

FAITH.   Shame her ?

RUDDLE. Listen. That flask contains potato-wine, and some o' the strongest potato-wine as was ever brewed. I reckon I've a stomach for liquor, but one glass o' that t'other night, and 'twas just as if somebody had given me a clout with a mallet.

FAITH. Yes, but why give it to Aunt Prudence?

RUDDLE. Don't you see? If she gets drunk afore the Colonel's wife and the schoolmistress, 'twill be all over the village in no time. They've pretty long tongues, the pair of 'em, in spite of all their *dear* Mrs. So-and-so and *dear* Mrs. Thingumy-bob!

FAITH. Yes, but what good is that going to do?

RUDDLE. What good? Why, once it gets round that your Aunt's an ine— an ineb— (*giving it up*) —drunken old woman, everybody'll be arter cutting her dead. People'll be pointing their finger at her in the village. A proud woman like her couldn't stand that. She'll pack her bags and be off in no time.

BOB. Ned, you're a genius!

RUDDLE. I'm glad somebody recognises it. (*He crosses to the window and looks out over to the R.*)

BOB. How's it going, Ned? Can you see them?

RUDDLE. Yes. They're on the lawn there.

FAITH. Have they got it yet?

RUDDLE. I think so. Yes, there's Cicely just coming away now. Good girl! She's been right smart with it, hasn't she?

FAITH. What about Aunt Prudence—is she drink-ing hers?

RUDDLE. Can't rightly tell. She's got her back towards me. I can see Loveday and the Missus though, they seem to be getting rid o' theirs. Aye, Loveday's praising it to your Aunt, I can tell by the way she's talking!

FAITH. Well—and what do we do now?

BOB. Just wait for developments, I suppose.

RUDDLE (*leaving window and coming back to them*). We shan't have to wait long.

FAITH. Why, Ned, does it act sudden?

RUDDLE. Instantaneous! At least, it were in my case—and I'm pretty hardened. With her not being used to it, it'll rush to her head in a flash.

FAITH (*seriously*). Wait a minute! You're forgetting something, surely?

RUDDLE. What's that?

FAITH. The tea. When Aunt Prudence tastes it, she'll know there's something wrong with it right away!

BOB. Yes, of course! And then she'll simply leave it alone. You ought to have thought of that, Ned!

RUDDLE. But I did think about it, and that's where the genius comes in.

BOB. How?

RUDDLE. Don't you remember what she said just now?

BOB. What about?

RUDDLE. The tea. "It's special tea," she said. "A new blend from my cousin in Ceylon. I haven't even tried it myself yet"—that's the important bit —"*I haven't tried it myself yet.*" Now do you see?

BOB. I've got it! She'll think it's a new flavour?

RUDDLE. Exactly! If she's had none before, she can't know what to expect.

FAITH. But suppose she doesn't like it?

RUDDLE. She'll like it all right. I did—till after I'd got it down! Besides, with the others sitting round there all saying how good her fancy stuff is, she couldn't for shame to leave it, even if it were rat-poison!

(*Several female voices raised in shrill laughter are suddenly heard outside.*)

RUDDLE. There you are! It's working, see!

FAITH. Sounds a bit funny to me. Why should they all be laughing?

RUDDLE. At your Aunt. They'll have to laugh now, being a bit polite-like. But wait till they get outside this gate, their tongues'll be wagging faster than fiddlers' elbows !

(*Another gale of laughter blows up.* FAITH *crosses to the window and looks out over to the R.*)

FAITH. I believe you're right, Ned. She's coming this way now. Looks a bit under the weather too.

(*The laughter blows up again. The door at the back opens and* PRUDENCE *enters. She is trying to retain her composure and dignity, but she is obviously slightly "under the influence."*)

PRUDENCE. Most disgushting ! Most disgushting behaviour ! Never seen anything so disgushting in all my life. Musht go and lie down. Yes, that's it. Musht go and lie down for a little while. (*She moves, not too steadily, towards the stairs.*)

BOB. Is there anything I can do to help you, ma'am ?

PRUDENCE. You ? No, young man, I can quite well look after myself ! (*Catching sight of* RUDDLE.) Ruddle !

RUDDLE. Here !

PRUDENCE. Ruddle ! I've a good mind to leave this place at once !

RUDDLE. Shall I be helping you to pack then ?

PRUDENCE. Pack ? Pack ? Wha' for ?

RUDDLE. If you're leaving.

PRUDENCE. Leaving ? Who said anything about leaving ? After thish I simply can't leave !

RUDDLE
BOB   } (*together*). CAN'T LEAVE ?
FAITH

PRUDENCE. Certainly not ! It'sh my bounden duty to stay here now to put an end to such disgushting behaviour ! (*She moves off up the stairs.*)

Disgushting! Never saw anything so disgushting Must go and lie down—— Yes, that'sh it—— Must go—— (*She disappears.*)

BOB. Ned Ruddle. There's something gone wrong here!

(*The gale of laughter blows up again.*)

RUDDLE. Just a minute! (*He crosses and opens the door R.*) Cicely!

CICELY (*entering*). Yes, Ned Ruddle?

RUDDLE (*remaining R. with* CICELY). Did you do what I told you?

CICELY. Yes. I've earned my half-crown, I reckon.

RUDDLE. Did you put it in her cup?

CICELY. No, and there's where I earned it. You see, I had to use my wits.

RUDDLE. What happened?

CICELY. Well, it didn't quite work out as *you* planned. I took the four cups out into the garden, same as I always do. I was just planting the one wi' the stuff in in front o' Miss Hannacott, when she turns on me. "Cicely," she says, "how dare you bring the tea like this! It'll be cold," she says, "You go and fetch four clean cups and the tea-pot and we'll pour it ourselves!"

RUDDLE (*grimly*). Fa-ancy tha-at!

CICELY. Well, I had to do something to make sure o' my half-crown. So I did the only thing I could think of!

RUDDLE. What was that?

CICELY (*proudly*). I put it in the tea-pot!

RUDDLE. WHAT?

BOB. IN THE TEA-POT?

CICELY. Yes—all of it. Look! (*She produces the empty flask from her apron-pocket.*)

RUDDLE (*moving over to C.*). Holy saints and sinners!

(*The gale of laughter blows up louder outside. The door at the back opens slowly, and* MISS LOVEDAY *appears, holding a fairly large tea-pot. She is definitely "under the weather."*)

LOVEDAY. Shishely! (*Hic.*) Shishely!
CICELY (*Going up to her*). Yes'm?
LOVEDAY. (*Hic!*) Another POT OF TEA, PLEASH!
CICELY (*taking the pot, and staring at* RUDDLE *in blank amazement*). FA-ANCY THA-AT!

(LOVEDAY *wags her finger at the astonished* BOB *and* RUDDLE, *laughs foolishly, then begins to stagger away singing. The gale of laughter blows up again.* FAITH *rushes out after her. As* RUDDLE *sheepishly draws the pound note from his pocket and hands it back to* BOB: —

the CURTAIN falls.

ACT TWO.

SCENE: *The Living-room of the Hannacott Farm-house, as before.*
TIME: *Evening, two days later.*

The curtain rises on the same setting as seen in ACT I. Everything is as before, save that the window-curtains are drawn, and a pair of heavy curtains shut out our view of the landing at the bottom of the stairs. A lamp stands in the centre of the table, presumably the only source of light in the room.

FAITH HANNACOTT *is discovered pacing up and down. She is obviously trying hard to learn her part, and though she holds the open book behind her back, she refers to it from time to time with a gesture of annoyance.*

Suddenly the door over on the R. opens, and CICELY *enters. She carries a tray of plates, butter, cheese and biscuits. She removes a white tablecloth from the tray and proceeds to spread it over the table.*

FAITH. What's this, Cicely? Setting for supper! Why, we haven't even started yet.

CICELY. Miss Hannacott's orders, Miss. She said 'twas to be got ready before anyone arrived.

FAITH. I see. (*Coming up to examine tray.*) What have we got?

CICELY. Cheese and biscuits.

FAITH. Hm! Not very exciting?

CICELY. No, Miss. Miss Hannacott said 'twould be better.

FAITH. Better?

CICELY. Seeing as there's so many expected.

FAITH. The old stinge! (*Taking a biscuit and munching it.*) And what do we have to drink—tea?

37

CICELY. No fear, Miss! Since that affair I'd sooner serve your Aunt with a glass o' beer than a cup o' tea.

FAITH (*maliciously*). Or even potato-wine, perhaps?

CICELY. Don't mention it, Miss.

FAITH. Do you think she suspects?

CICELY. She never said nothing. All the same, every time she looks at me, I feels as if her eyes were boring right through me.

FAITH. A guilty conscience, Cicely?

CICELY. Oh, I know I shouldn't have done it. Still, I didn't mean no harm. 'Twould never have happened but for that Ned Ruddle—the old villain!

FAITH. Yes, it was very wrong, Cicely. Still, if it comes to that, we are all as guilty. I was as much a party to it as anyone else.

CICELY. 'Twas seeing the Missus that way as upset me most. Every time we got her down in bed, she was up again prancing on the mattress, and saying as she'd dance Pavlova off her feet any day.

FAITH (*sitting in arm-chair over L.*). Yes, it was terrible, wasn't it?

CICELY. And then poor Miss Loveday and the Colonel's wife.

FAITH. I'm afraid I was too busy attending to Mother and Aunt Prudence. What happened to them?

CICELY. Well, Ned and Mr. Sladen managed to get 'em loaded up into the trap, and Ned started to take 'em home. But then they began to sing at the top o' their voices!

FAITH. Good gracious!

CICELY. Aye, and Ned had to drive 'em round the lanes till they fell asleep, afore he durst take 'em through the village.

FAITH. Altogether a very expensive way of earning half-a-crown, eh, Cicely?

CICELY. That's just the trouble, Miss.

FAITH. What is?

CICELY. The half-crown! I didn't get it.

FAITH. Didn't get it? (*Going C.*)

CICELY. No. Ned Ruddle said as I hadn't carried out the bargain satisfactorily—so he refuses to pay me!

FAITH (*approaching* CICELY). Don't worry, Cicely. I'll see that you get it.

CICELY. Thank you, Miss. Not that I really expects it—not after the trouble I've caused.

FAITH. By the way—how is Aunt Prudence to-day? I'm afraid I've been too busy to see much of her.

CICELY. Just the same, Miss. Just the same as she was yesterday. Only a shade more on the attack, as you might say.

FAITH. *She* soon came round, didn't she? (*Coming down L. of table.*)

CICELY. Aye. Ned says she ain't no beginner. Says it ain't the first time she's had liquor down and kept it down!

FAITH. You mustn't take any notice of Ned. He's very bitter.

CICELY. Fa-ancy tha-at! Well he needn't be. He's half-a-crown better off!

FAITH. No, Cicely. Seventeen and sixpence out of pocket!

CICELY. I'm afraid I don't——?

FAITH. No, of course you don't. Never mind!

CICELY. Very good, Miss.

(CICELY *proceeds to put the plates from the tray on to the table.* FAITH *continues to memorise her part.*)

CICELY (*picking up tray, and preparing to depart*). Will the Missus be wanting anything?

FAITH. No, I don't think so, Cicely.

CICELY. Is she feeling better now?

FAITH. Much better, thanks. As a matter of

fact, she's decided to get up.   She'll be down shortly.

CICELY.   I'm glad o' that!   How's the part going, Miss?   (*Coming over L. and peeping at* FAITH'S *script.*)

FAITH.   Not too well, I'm afraid.   When I look at the book I seem to know it; but as soon as I start trying to act it—it all flies out of my head.

CICELY.   It'd be just the same with me.   Except the love-bits of course.

FAITH.   The love-bits?   So you think you could manage those?

CICELY.   Oh, yes!   You don't have to learn them. All you need to do is gag 'em.

FAITH.   Gag 'em?

CICELY.   Yes.   I read all about it in the " Film Weekly."   Some of the picture-stars don't learn any lines when they're doing a love-scene.   They just says whatever comes into their heads.

FAITH.   Really?   How interesting!

CICELY.   Course, it doesn't always work.

FAITH   No?

CICELY.   No.   I read o' one case where the girl lay nestling in the fellow's arms, looking up into his eyes for ever so long.   Then she suddenly whips out: " Good heavens!   I forgot to order the fish for dinner! "

(FAITH *laughs.   At that moment there is a sharp, distinctive knock, obviously a pre-arranged signal, as it goes:* " Pom-po-po-pom-pom-POM! Pom! ")

CICELY.   Good gracious!   Here's the first of 'em. Shall I let 'em in, Miss?

FAITH.   No, off you go, Cicely.   I think I know who this one is.

(CICELY *exits via the door R.*   FAITH *crosses to the back door and opens it, revealing* BOB SLADEN.

He carries his book under his arm, and wears his best clothes.)

BOB. Faith ! (*He steps inside and looks around.*) All alone ?

(FAITH *nods.*)

BOB (*moving towards her*). Good ! Then I'm the first ?

FAITH (*coyly, and slipping away from him over to the R.*). You ought to be, Mr. Sladen—considering that rehearsal's called for eight o'clock, and it's not quite ten to, yet.

BOB (*playing up*). Exactly, Miss Hannacott. That is precisely what I intended ! (*Going L.*)

FAITH. And for why, Mr. Sladen ?

BOB. Private rehearsal, Miss Hannacott.

FAITH. Is that necessary ?

BOB. Absolutely !

FAITH. Then you're not word-perfect ?

BOB (*crossing and taking her in his arms*). No—but action-perfect. (*They are both C. in front of table. He kisses her, then releases her and speaks mock-seriously.*) There ! What did you think about that ?

FAITH (*also mock-serious, in an attitude of deep deliberation*). Good !—but you'll improve.

BOB. With practice ?

FAITH. No—with experience !

(*They both laugh.*)

BOB (*resting against front of table*). But seriously—how's things ?

FAITH (*following suit*). Improving—but none too good.

BOB. Your Aunt—how's she ?

FAITH. Just the same as ever.

BOB. She's got over it by now ?

FAITH. Oh, yes. She was as sprightly as ever yesterday morning !

BOB. Then she doesn't suspect?

FAITH. I don't think so. She's had the canister of tea thrown away. So that's a good sign, isn't it?

BOB. Yes, I suppose it is. And your Mother—how's she?

FAITH. Much better now, thanks. But she was very poorly yesterday.

BOB. I'm so sorry. Ned Ruddle made a fine mess of things, the fool!

FAITH. Yes, thanks to poor Cicely—and another couple of fools besides!

BOB (*standing*). I suppose you're right, dear. Still, you would have laughed if you'd seen the Colonel's wife and Miss Loveday standing up in the trap and bawling out "Just a Song at Twilight," with their arms round one another's necks.

FAITH. It must have been dreadful. I do hope they're both all right.

BOB. Well, they both turned up at service last night.

FAITH. How did they look?

BOB. Pretty green! Still, it should have worn off by now. They'll be along to-night, you see.

FAITH (*also rising*). In which case we shan't have much longer to ourselves.

BOB (*with a wink*). I understand!—(*about to embrace her*)—then we'd better get on——

FAITH (*dodging him and crossing over*). With the rehearsal! Yes! You'll need your book.

BOB (*stuffing book into pocket*). I shan't! I know it!

FAITH. All of it?

BOB. No! The bit that matters.

FAITH. We'll see.

BOB. All right. You kick off.

FAITH (*retaining book*). Ready?

BOB. Yes!

FAITH (*reading*). "James, you must go now. If my Father were to find you here, there'd be a terrible scene."

Bob. "Patricia, I'm not afraid. I—I'd—(*stumbling*)—

Faith (*whispering*). "Dare ! "

Bob. That's it ! "I'd dare far worse things than that—to be with you." (*He slips his arm around her.*)

Faith. "If only I could be sure of you. Sure that you really cared.

Bob. "Cared ? "—(*He takes her in his arms.*)—"Patricia—I love you."

Faith. "Do you really mean that, James ? "

Bob. "Mean it ? Ever since I first came to this house, sleep-walking——"

Faith.. Sleeping—waking !

Bob. Oh, yes, that's better ! "Sleeping, waking, the only thing in your thoughts has been the vision of me."

Faith. WHAT ?

Bob. Never mind. It'll do for now: "Patricia, I love you ! "

Faith. "And I love you too ! "

(*They are just preparing to kiss, when the door at the back opens, and* NED RUDDLE *appears.*)

RUDDLE (*disgusted*). What, again !

(*He turns to go out, pulling the door behind him.*)

FAITH. It's all right, Ned. You can come inside.

BOB (*going L.*). Yes—we shall need our butler, you know.

RUDDLE. Aye, then I'd best stop out here and do what a good butler should do.

BOB. What's that ?

RUDDLE. Let you know when anybody's coming.

FAITH. Don't be silly, Ned! We were only rehearsing.

RUDDLE. That's what old Sam Johnson said in the witness-box. But it cost him fifty pound !

BOB. What for ?

RUDDLE. Breach o' promise !

FAITH (*front of table*). Take no notice of him, Bob. He's still sore about the tea business.

RUDDLE (*entering and closing the door*). Sore? And well I might be! A cast-iron scheme it was! What do you think, Bob Sladen?

BOB. A good idea that didn't work.

RUDDLE (*coming down R.*). Aye—and good potato-wine as did!

FAITH. I see. It's the loss of that that's upsetting you?

RUDDLE (*sitting R. of table*). Not altogether, Miss. I got some sort o' recompense, as you might say.

FAITH. Where from?

RUDDLE. The canister o' tea.

FAITH. How?

RUDDLE. Well, you see, yesterday morning Miss Hannacott gave me the tin, nigh on four pounds there was in it, and told me to throw it away.

BOB. And what did you do with it?

RUDDLE. Threw it away.

BOB. Where?

RUDDLE. At the "Foresters' Arms." Raffled it off for six shillings!

BOB. And do you call that throwing it away?

RUDDLE. Wouldn't you? At eighteen-pence a pound!

FAITH. I see. So there's no excuse now for you not paying Cicely that half-crown?

RUDDLE. What half-crown?

FAITH. The one you owe her—for helping to make three innocent ladies drunk!

RUDDLE (*rising and going R.*). I don't owe her no half-crown! She didn't do proper what I told her.

FAITH (*rising from front of table*). Oh yes, she did! And you're going to pay up. I promised her that you shall.

RUDDLE. Very well, Miss. On one condition only!

FAITH. What's that?

RUDDLE. She must wait until I can pay her out of that pound I'm going to earn.

BOB. *Going* to earn? So you haven't given up the idea?

RUDDLE. Given up? I haven't started yet!

FAITH. Then it's only the pound you're after, Ned Ruddle?

RUDDLE. Pound be blowed! It's the six years as is frightening me! I want to get rid o' that woman, same as you. The pound is only a' added incentive. Like marrying an ugly woman wi' money!

BOB. I think we'd better let it drop—after what's happened.

RUDDLE. What? Do you fancy the idea o' courting for six years?

BOB. No—not likely!

RUDDLE. And you, Miss?

FAITH. Well—no, I——

RUDDLE. There you are, then. It's got to be done!

BOB. Yes, but look here—no more tea business!

RUDDLE. No fear! What do you take me for? Never strike in the same place twice, that's fatal!

BOB. Then what do you suggest?

RUDDLE. Leave it to me.

FAITH. But we did that last time—and look what happened!

RUDDLE (*coming back and sitting R. of table*). Yes, but the next won't fail. Third time pays for all, they say.

BOB. Third? But this is only the second.

RUDDLE. Not it! Ned Ruddle don't let no grass grow under his feet. The second attempt was yesterday.

FAITH. And was it a success?

RUDDLE (*with a shrug of his shoulders*). She's still here!

FAITH. Yes, but do tell us what happened.

RUDDLE. Well, it was this way. I said to myself: " Ned Ruddle, you've tried to shame her away, and drawn a blank. So what's the next thing on the carpet? Why! Frighten her away to be sure!

FAITH. Frighten her!

RUDDLE. Yes. So I sets down to think out how it could be done. Finally I hits on the very thing.

BOB. Well?

RUDDLE. I went and dug out young Harry Greensmith. He's got a couple o' ferrets, and soon I was back here with as bonny a rat as you've ever seen in your life.

FAITH. Good heavens! What did you do?

RUDDLE. I sent Cicely to tell Miss Hannacott as she was wanted in the dairy. As soon as I saw her coming, I opened the bag, chucked the rat in, and slammed the door to. Then I ran round to the window to watch.

BOB. And what did she do?

RUDDLE. Marched straight in, gave one look at it, and then—what do you think she did?

BOB. Screamed and ran!

FAITH. Fainted!

RUDDLE. Neither. She grabbed the Master's old shot-gun from the corner and blew it to blazes!

BOB (laughing). Good for her! She's got courage, anyway.

RUDDLE. Aye. I wouldn't have cared so very much, but just at the moment she fired—it were hiding behind my best boots!

FAITH. So that was why Mother said she heard a shot?

RUDDLE. Aye, and that's why I'm wearing these! (*He displays a pair of decrepit boots, heavily caked with mud.*)

BOB. Then the frightening idea's not much use, Ned. You'll have to give that up.

RUDDLE. I'm not so sure o' that.

BOB. What? Remember what you just said: " Never strike in the same place twice."

RUDDLE. Aye, but there's different ways o' frightening. A woman may be as bold as brass if it's something as she can see. But supposing it's something as she can't see? How about that?

BOB. What are you driving at?

RUDDLE. Put it this way. She may not be frightened o' the natural; but how about if it's the super-natural?

FAITH. Do you mean to say you're thinking of dressing up as a ghost or something?

RUDDLE (*rising*). What! After seeing the way as she handles a shot-gun? Not likely!

FAITH. Then what *are* you getting at?

RUDDLE. I dunno, quite. (*Looking at picture above stairs.*) I've been wondering if—— (*He crosses to the picture and examines it; mounts the steps and surveys it from the back as well.*)

FAITH. What on earth are you doing, Ned?

RUDDLE (*pre-occupied*). Hm! It might! The nail's gone straight through.

BOB. What's that got to do with it?

RUDDLE (*excitedly*). By jove! Yes, I've got it!

FAITH. What?

RUDDLE. Just wait and you'll see. I've always hated that picture, but it's going to be a blessing in disguise!

BOB. How?

RUDDLE. It's going to get rid of her. (*Chuckling.*) Frighten her with her own face! That's justice with a vengeance, that is.

FAITH. You've said that twice before.

RUDDLE. Aye, but I can taste that pound this time.

BOB. Taste it?

RUDDLE. Reduced to pints!

FAITH. Ned Ruddle! I insist that you tell us what you intend to do.

(BOB *sits L. of table* FAITH *resting against table.*)

RUDDLE (*coming R. of table*).   Very well, Miss.
To-night, when we're all setting round afore going
to bed, I'm going to——

(*But he gets no further, for there is rather a timid
knocking at the door, back.   FAITH signs to
RUDDLE to be quiet.   She open the door, and
MISS LOVEDAY stands revealed.*)

LOVEDAY.   My dear Faith.   Just in time for the
rehearsal, I hope.   Eight o'clock, we said, wasn't it ?
FAITH.   That's right, Miss Loveday. Come inside !
LOVEDAY.   Thank you ever so.   Ah, Mr. Sladen !
You're an early bird !   And Mr. Ruddle, too.   I do
so hope you're going to like being a butler.   Let me
see, you've never taken anything like this before ?
RUDDLE (*down R.*).   Only once, Ma'am.
LOVEDAY.   What was that ?
RUDDLE.   Castor-oil !
LOVEDAY (*feigning to laugh*).   Ah, Mr. Ruddle !
(*To BOB.*)   He's such a wit, isn't he ?   (*To FAITH.*)
And what about your Mother and the dear Aunt ?
They're quite—(*she coughs self-consciously*)—quite
well, I hope ?
FAITH.   Oh, yes.   They're both well enough now.
Though they have been a little off-colour.
LOVEDAY.   Yes, I must admit that I have been
a little run-down myself.   Still, what can you ex-
pect ?   It was awfully close over the week-end,
wasn't it ?
RUDDLE.   It were on Saturday !

(MISS LOVEDAY *throws him a doubtful glance, but
RUDDLE never moves a muscle.*)

LOVEDAY.   Well, we must be getting along with
the rehearsal, mustn't we ?
FAITH.   Shall I call Mother and Aunt Prudence ?
LOVEDAY.   If you would be so kind, dear.   Time
presses !

(FAITH *exits up the stairs.*)

Ah ! Time, Mr. Ruddle.   It governs all our lives,
doesn't it ?   Think of all the sayings about Time.
" Time is a great healer "—" Time and Tide wait
for no man "—" Time—

RUDDLE.   " Gentlemen, please ! "

LOVEDAY (*feigning to laugh*).   Of course, Mr.
Ruddle.   But I don't hear that as much perhaps
as you do.

RUDDLE.   Naturally, ma'am.   You being a staunch
teetotaler !

LOVEDAY (*throwing him another nervous glance*).
Oh, quite, quite !   Dear me !   I can't think what
can have happened to the dear Colonel's wife.
(*Rather obviously.*)   I wonder, Mr. Sladen, if you'd
step down to the road, and see if you can see anything of her ?

BOB.   Certainly, Miss Loveday.

(BOB *exits through door, back.* RUDDLE *crosses L.*)

LOVEDAY (*coughing, after a slight pause*).   Mr.
Ruddle ?

RUDDLE.   Yes'm.

LOVEDAY.   I hope I may speak in confidence ?

RUDDLE.   Absolutely, ma'am.

LOVEDAY.   And that I can trust to your discretion
concerning a recent—er—rather regrettable and un-
fortunate happening concerning myself ?

RUDDLE.   I beg your pardon, M'm ?

LOVEDAY.   I refer to the distressing incident of
last Saturday morning.

RUDDLE.   Oh, that !

LOVEDAY.   Yes.   Mr. Ruddle, I am most anxious
that you should have no false impressions regard-
ing my behaviour, extraordinary as it may have
appeared.   I want to assure you that I was not—
er—well, not what I may have seemed to be.

RUDDLE.   I quite understand.

LOVEDAY.   I don't know whatever came over me.
It must have been the heat or something.   I
suddenly felt as if—as if——

RUDDLE.   As if you were a hen laying its first egg !

LOVEDAY.   Quite, quite !   Mr. Ruddle.   I shall be eternally grateful for the way you—er—so kindly saw me home.   I hope no-one saw, er——?

RUDDLE.   Not a soul !   I took good care o' that.

LOVEDAY.   I'm so glad !   That was so thoughtful of you.   Not that there was anything wrong ; but people are apt to jump to conclusions, aren't they ?

RUDDLE.   They are !

LOVEDAY.   So no one will ever know anything about my—er—attack ; that is, of course, unless *you* were to——

RUDDLE.   What *me*, M'm ?   No fear !   I'd never breathe a word to a soul !

LOVEDAY (*with a sigh of relief*).   There ; I knew I could trust you, dear Mr. Ruddle.   And now perhaps you will accept this.   (*She hands him two coins.*)   Not for any ulterior motive, you know. Just as a slight recognition of your kindliness in seeing me home.

RUDDLE.   Five shillings !   Oh, thank you, M'm ! Thank you very much indeed !

LOVEDAY.   Then you quite understand, Mr. Ruddle ?

RUDDLE.   Perfectly !

(MISS LOVEDAY *breathes another sigh of satisfaction. The door, back, opens and* BOB *enters.   He leaves the door ajar.*)

BOB.   She's here, ma'am, now !   She's just turned the corner.

LOVEDAY.   Thank you, Mr. Sladen !   Oh, by the way, I've just remembered.   There's one or two little things in your part that I should like to have a word with you about, in private, before we begin.

BOB.   Why certainly, Miss Loveday.

RUDDLE (*moving*).   Do you want me to shift, M'm ?

LOVEDAY (*moving to door L.*).   No, Mr. Ruddle.

(*Opening door.*)   Ah, there's a light in here.   Come along, Mr. Sladen !   Only a moment or two, that's all.

BOB.   Very good, Ma'am.

(*She exits, followed by* BOB.   RUDDLE *stares at the two half-crowns in his hand, scratches his head, and chuckles deeply.   A moment or two later,* MRS. MIDDLETON-JONES *appears in the open door-way at the back.   She gives a timid tap.*)

MIDDLETON-JONES.   I do hope I am not intruding ?

RUDDLE (*who has gone over L. of table*).   Not at all, ma'am.   Step inside !

MIDDLETON-JONES.   All alone, Mr. Ruddle ?

RUDDLE.   They're all here.   Some there (*he indicates L. with his thumb*) and some up there ! (*He indicates R. towards the stairs with the other thumb.*)

MIDDLETON-JONES (*coming down R. of table*). Then before we are disturbed, I should like to— (*She coughs*)—Mr. Ruddle !

RUDDLE.   Yes'm ?

MIDDLETON-JONES.   I hope I may speak in confidence?

RUDDLE.   Absolutely, ma'am.

MIDDLETON-JONES.   Then with reference to that unpleasant little affair of Saturday morning last, I——

RUDDLE.   I know, ma'am.   (*Almost reciting.*) You were taken ill—it was the heat—I took you home—nobody saw you—I ain't said a word—and I've forgotten all about it.

MIDDLETON-JONES.   Oh, how tactful, Mr. Ruddle ! How extremely tactful of you.   If only the dear Colonel were as tactful as—— But there ! What am I saying ?   Mr. Ruddle, if you will accept this small token of my indebtedness, I shall be extremely grateful.   (*She hands him a note.*)

RUDDLE.   Ten shillings !   Really, ma'am, it's too

good of you. If ever I can do anything to
oblige——?

MIDDLETON-JONES. Perhaps there is just one little
thing you might be able to do for me, Mr. Ruddle

RUDDLE. Anything, Ma'am, anything !

MIDDLETON-JONES. I should be glad if you could
find out for me——

RUDDLE. Yes'm ?

MIDDLETON-JONES. What brand of tea Miss Hannacott uses.

(But any further observation by RUDDLE *is cut short
by the entrance of* TILDA HANNACOTT *from the
stairs, followed by* FAITH.)*

TILDA. Mrs. Middleton-Jones ! Faith didn't tell
me you were here.

MIDDLETON-JONES. Dear Mrs. Hannacott ! I do
hope we're not putting you to too much trouble
with our rehearsal ?

*(*PRUDENCE *appears at the head of the stairs. She
carries her book.)*

TILDA. No trouble at all ! It's the least I can
do——

PRUDENCE. *We* can do, Tilda !

TILDA *(flustered)*. Yes, of course. I mean it's
the least we can do to help in every way possible.

*(*TILDA *moves over L. to fireplace.)*

MIDDLETON-JONES. Thank you—both ! I do hope
you are keeping well, Miss Hannacott ?

PRUDENCE *(coldly)*. There is no reason why I
shouldn't be, is there ?

MIDDLETON-JONES *(awkwardly)*. Oh, no, certainly not ! That is—of course not, dear Miss
Hannacott !

PRUDENCE. Very well, then. Hadn't we better
be making a start?—*(to* FAITH)—Where's Miss Loveday ? I thought you told me she was here ?

FAITH. She was—a few moments ago.

RUDDLE (*pointing L.*). She's in yonder.

PRUDENCE. And what is she doing in there, pray ?

RUDDLE. Having an affair wi' young Bob Sladen !

PRUDENCE. WHAT ?

RUDDLE. Rehearsing him, then—if you wants it plainer.

PRUDENCE. Ruddle !   Never let me hear you make a foolish remark like that again !

RUDDLE. But I didn't mean——

PRUDENCE. No matter !   Always remember that a man's tongue sows the seeds of all evil.

RUDDLE. Aye, but a woman's mind is where they're bedded out !

PRUDENCE. That's quite enough !

(*The door L. opens, and* MISS LOVEDAY *and* BOB SLADEN *enter.*)

LOVEDAY. Ah ! good-evening, everybody.   So sorry if we've kept you waiting.   Mr. Sladen and I were just settling one or two little affairs——

RUDDLE (*triumphantly*). There !   What did I tell you ?

(PRUDENCE *darts him a venomous glance.*)

PRUDENCE. Well, Miss Loveday, now that we're all here, don't you think we'd better begin ?

LOVEDAY (*coming to L.C.*).   Ah, but that's the trouble.   You see, we're not all here.

PRUDENCE. Who's missing ?

LOVEDAY. Mr. Meacock.

PRUDENCE. Meacock ?

LOVEDAY. Yes.   He's the landlord at the "Foresters' Arms."   A bit rough and ready, but a good sort.   He always helps us out.

PRUDENCE. Then why isn't he here now ?

LOVEDAY. Well, you see, he finds it rather diffi-cult to get out in the evening.   Says it's his busiest time.

RUDDLE. It is !

LOVEDAY. Still, he's promised to come over here in the afternoon when he's shut, and go through his part then.

PRUDENCE. H'm! Very considerate of him.

MIDDLETON-JONES. Oh, you needn't worry about him. He's a quick learner. Always has his part off before the first rehearsal, hasn't he, dear?

LOVEDAY. Yes. Still it does make it a bit awkward, especially as he is in two of the plays.

PRUDENCE. Two plays?

LOVEDAY. Yes. He plays the Father in "Love and a Locksmith," and he plays opposite you, Mrs. Hannacott, in "Age Shall Not Wither."

TILDA. Dear me! I do hope we shall get on all right?

LOVEDAY. Oh, you'll manage. By the way, we don't really need you to-night, Mrs. Hannacott; that is—unless you care to watch us?

TILDA (*a little uncertain as to whether she is being dismissed*). Well—I——

PRUDENCE. Certainly! You sit down and watch us, Tilda.

TILDA (*meekly*). Yes, Prudence. (*She sits over on L.*)

PRUDENCE. And now—isn't it time we were making a start?

LOVEDAY. At once, at once! If you've all got your books ready, we'll start at Page One.

(*They all open up books.*)

Now, this will do nicely for the set as it stands. The table here—that's right. The window at the back. Oh, there's an armchair over here. Mr. Sladen—do you mind?

(BOB *takes the wicker-chair from the L. and places it over R.*)

That's it! Now, Miss Hannacott. You are sitting by the table.

.(PRUDENCE *sits.   The others go towards the back.
MISS LOVEDAY comes well forward, back to the
audience, taking command.)*

MIDDLETON-JONES.   One moment, dear !   What
about Mr. Meacock's part ?
LOVEDAY.   Oh, yes !   Mr. Ruddle ?
RUDDLE.   Yes'm ?
LOVEDAY.   Will you read Mr. Meacock's part,
please ?
RUDDLE.   WHAT ?
LOVEDAY.   Mr. Meacock's part—the father !
RUDDLE.   But I'm the butler !
LOVEDAY.   Yes, I know.   But you haven't much.
You can manage this as well.
RUDDLE.   But I don't know how it's done !
LOVEDAY.   Nonsense !   It's quite simple.   I want
you to imagine you are Miss Hannacott's husband.
RUDDLE (*sotto voce*).   Heaven forbid !
PRUDENCE.   What ?
RUDDLE.   I said it'll have to be did.
PRUDENCE.   All right, then.   Get on with it !
LOVEDAY.   Now the curtain goes up !   You, Mr.
Ruddle, are seated in the armchair.—(*He sits*)—
That's right !   Now, are you all ready ?
OMNES.   Yes !
LOVEDAY.   Then off we go !   The curtain is up.
There is silence for a few moments, then—the butler
enters !
RUDDLE.   What ?
LOVEDAY.   The butler enters.   That's you !
RUDDLE.   Yes, but I'm here !
LOVEDAY.   No, that's Mr. Meacock.
RUDDLE.   Oh !   (*He rises, goes to the back, and
attempts a clumsy entrance.*)   " Mrs. Fotheringay,
my lord."
LOVEDAY.   Oh, no, Mr. Ruddle !   That won't do !
A butler would never walk like that !
RUDDLE.   He would if he had these boots on !
(*He displays a dilapidated sole.*)

LOVEDAY. Never mind, Mr. Ruddle.   Just once more, if you don't mind, please?

RUDDLE (*repeating entrance as before*). "Mrs. Fotheringay, my lord."

LOVEDAY. All right.   Carry on!

(*Slight pause.*)

Go on, Mr. Ruddle!

RUDDLE. 'Taint me!

LOVEDAY. It is!

RUDDLE (*pointing to book*).   Lord Fairfield—it says.

LOVEDAY. That's you!

RUDDLE. Me?

LOVEDAY. Mr. Meacock!

RUDDLE. Oh!   (*He crosses to chair and sits.*)

RUDDLE (*reading*). "Do you know her, my dear?"

PRUDENCE (*reading*). "There's something familiar about the name, John."

RUDDLE. "Hm!   Better see what she wants. Show her in, Thompson."

(RUDDLE *jumps up and waddles to the back.*)

"Very good, my lord." (*He pretends to exit, then waddles back to the chair.*) "Agnes, my dear. Where's Patricia?"

PRUDENCE. "I couldn't say, John.   Out riding— I suppose!"

RUDDLE. "Agnes, I've felt rather worried lately over crossing to the fireplace——."

LOVEDAY. Stop! Stop, Mr. Ruddle! You don't say that! That's a stage-direction. You cross to the fireplace on the word "over"—that's all!

RUDDLE. Oh! All right. I'll have another smack at it. (*Repeating.*) "Agnes, I've felt rather worried lately over" (*He stops and waddles over to the fireplace L.*) "over our daughter, Patricia."

LOVEDAY. No, Mr. Ruddle.   To the fireplace— not there!

RUDDLE (*pointing to fireplace*). Well, what's this ?

LOVEDAY (*going and bringing him over R.*). No, you don't understand. The fireplace is over here (*pointing R.*). It isn't really here, you see ; but this is where it is !

RUDDLE (*scratching his head*). Eh ?

LOVEDAY. I say it isn't really here—but this is where it is.

RUDDLE (*looking at her curiously*). Well, maybe you're right !

LOVEDAY. Yes. Now go straight on.

RUDDLE (*reading*). " From what I hear, Patricia has been making quite a fool of herself just lately."

PRUDENCE. " In what way, John ? "

RUDDLE. " She been going about with that young bounder, James Fenton."

PRUDENCE. " James Fenton ? "

LOVEDAY. That's right, Miss Hannacott. A little more shocked though, if you can remember.

PRUDENCE. I'll remember. Go along, Ruddle !

RUDDLE (*entirely devoid of expression*). " Yes. James Fenton—of all people. I'd like to horse-whip the young monkey."

LOVEDAY. Stop ! Stop ! It says " furiously " in front of that. The whole speech wants to be bristling with anger, Mr. Ruddle.

RUDDLE. Me ?

LOVEDAY. Yes, you !

RUDDLE. But it wasn't me that said it.

LOVEDAY (*exasperated*). Then who was it ?

RUDDLE. Mr. Meacock !

LOVEDAY. Oh—of course—yes ! Well we'll leave it for now. Proceed from that point. Enter Thompson.

RUDDLE (*waddling to back*). " Mrs. Fotheringay, my lord." (*He waddles back to chair.*)

LOVEDAY. Enter Mrs. Fotheringay. (*Pause.*) MRS. FOTHERINGAY !

(*But there is no response from* MRS. MIDDLETON-JONES, *who is chatting pleasantly with* FAITH *on the settee at the back.*)

LOVEDAY.   Mrs. Middleton-Jones !

MIDDLETON-JONES (*looking up*).   Yes, dear ?

LOVEDAY.   This is your entrance.

MIDDLETON-JONES.   Really ?   Good gracious !   I beg your pardon.   (*Rising and fussing with book.*) I'm sorry to trouble you, dear, but I'm afraid I've forgotten—that is—would you mind telling me who I am ?

LOVEDAY.   Mrs. Fotheringay !

MIDDLETON-JONES (*blankly*).   Fotheringay ?   Oh, yes—of course !

PRUDENCE.   Do you mean to say that you don't know which part you're taking ?

MIDDLETON-JONES.   Well, you see,—foolish of me, I know,—but I haven't read the thing properly yet.

PRUDENCE (*sarcastically*).   Then you'd better start now, hadn't you ?

MIDDLETON-JONES.   Yes, of course.   What page, dear ?

LOVEDAY.   Two !

MIDDLETON-JONES.   Ah, yes.   I've got it!

PRUDENCE.   Then get on with it !

MIDDLETON-JONES   (*reading*).   " Good-evening, John.   Good-evening, Agnes ! "

PRUDENCE (*rising*).   " Clara !—You ? "

RUDDLE (*rising*).   What are you doing in my house ? "

MIDDLETON-JONES.   " Don't be alarmed, John.   I haven't come to steal you from Agnes."

PRUDENCE.   " Steal him from *me*—his wife ! "

MIDDLETON-JONES.   " Yes, my dear Agnes.   It would only be returning the compliment, wouldn't it ?   Seeing that you stole him from me ! "

RUDDLE.   " Get out of my house, woman ! "

MIDDLETON-JONES.   " Not so fast, John.   You were fine and handsome twenty-five years ago—you're fine and handsome still ! "

(FAITH *bursts out laughing.*)

LOVEDAY.   Silence, please !

MIDDLETON-JONES.   "But now you're cruel—yes, cruel !   You threw me on one side five and twenty years ago, but at last my turn has come ! "

RUDDLE.   "What do you mean ? "

MIDDLETON-JONES.   "Your daughter, Patricia. She loves young James Fenton.   She's going to marry him."

PRUDENCE.   "Never !   I would never consent ! "

MIDDLETON-JONES.   "No matter.   She *will* marry him, in spite of you both ! "

PRUDENCE.   "Even if she did.   What has this to do with you ? "

MIDDLETON-JONES.   "Everything.   James Fenton is my son ! "

PRUDENCE.   "WHAT ? "

MIDDLETON-JONES.   "JAMES FENTON IS MY SON ! MY SON — AND — (*Pointing to* RUDDLE)— . . . ! " (*Suddenly she realises and becomes very distressed.*) Oh, Miss Loveday !   Oh, no, no, no !   I couldn't do this !   Really—I don't know how you dare have asked me to play such a dreadful part !

LOVEDAY.   But you agreed to take the part.   You said you'd read it, and liked it.

MIDDLETON-JONES (*almost hysterical*)   I tell you it's a disgrace !   I've never been so insulted before ! What would the Colonel say—and the villagers ? (*Throwing down her book.*)   I refuse to take the part !   You horrible old woman, Loveday !   I resign !

RUDDLE (*trying to conciliate*).   Don't take it that way, ma'am.   It wouldn't be me really.   It'd be Mr. Meacock, you see, not me!

MIDDLETON-JONES (*with a horrified gasp*).   Oh ! (*She makes for the back door, head held high, and sails straight out, slamming it behind her. There is dead silence for a moment, then* RUDDLE *speaks.)*

RUDDLE. And they all lived happy ever after !

PRUDENCE. Now what are we going to do ?

LOVEDAY. Don't worry, Miss Hannacott. She'll come round. If she doesn't, we can always get someone else to play the part.

RUDDLE. Aye, a proper actress, maybe !

FAITH. It's her own fault. She ought to have read the part before.

LOVEDAY. Precisely ! And that is where she gave herself away.

BOB. I suppose this puts an end to rehearsal for to-night, then, Miss Loveday ?

LOVEDAY. Not at all ! Mrs. Hannacott can read the part for us, perhaps. (*To* TILDA.) What do you say ?

TILDA. Well—I—I——

PRUDENCE. Certainly ! Come along, Tilda, and read it !

TILDA. Very well.

(TILDA *rises and picks up the book from the floor.)*

LOVEDAY. We'll begin at ——

(*The door R. opens, and* CICELY *enters.)*

CICELY (*to* TILDA). If you please, Missus,——

PRUDENCE. Cicely ! *I* am here. You can address yourself to me.

CICELY. If you please, Ma'am, there's a boy at the back has brought a message for Miss Loveday.

LOVEDAY. Yes, Cicely. What is it ?

CICELY. He says one of the scouts over at the schoolroom has broken his arm, and will you please to come over at once.

LOVEDAY. Good gracious me ! I'll come immediately. I'm afraid that will mean the end of rehearsal for to-night. (*Crossing to door, back, she stops and looks at* TILDA.) Thank you so much, Mrs.—— (*Transferring her gaze to* PRUDENCE.) I mean, thank you so much, Miss Hannacott.

PRUDENCE. Won't you stay and have a little supper before you go ?

LOVEDAY. Thank you, no. I really must get back !

PRUDENCE. Just a cup of tea ? (*Hastily.*) I mean a glass of milk, perhaps ?

LOVEDAY. No, thanks. Some other time if you don't mind. Good-night, everybody, good-night !

(*She exits hastily via the back door. CICELY busies herself at the dresser.*)

FAITH. Well, that's a rehearsal—that was !

BOB. And we never even appeared.

RUDDLE (*sitting in armchair R.*). Neither did Sammy Meacock—yet he's got hisself into trouble !

PRUDENCE. Well, I suppose there's nothing else for it but to have some supper. You'll stay for a snack, Mr. Sladen ?

BOB. Please, Ma'am.

PRUDENCE. Most inconsiderate of those two women to rush away like that, especially when they could see the food on the table.

RUDDLE. Perhaps it were too much for 'em.

PRUDENCE (*missing the point*). What—biscuits and cheese ?

RUDDLE. No—the thoughts of it !

PRUDENCE. Ruddle ! (*She glares for a second, then turns to CICELY.*) Cicely !

CICELY. Yes'm.

PRUDENCE. Serve the milk, please. At once !

CICELY. Very good, Miss Hannacott.

(*She exits R. BOB and FAITH wander over to the window at the back.*)

PRUDENCE (*sitting L. of table*). Well, Tilda, what do you think of that Middleton-Jones woman now ?

TILDA. I really can't say. All very upsetting, wasn't it ?

PRUDENCE. Upsetting—fiddlesticks ! (*Helping*

herself to biscuits and cheese.) The woman doesn't know her own mind, that's all !

TILDA (*sitting behind table*). But she could hardly take a part like that, could she ? I mean, her being the Colonel's wife.

PRUDENCE. Then she ought to have declined it in the first place. I can't stand women like that ! Women who want to run the whole show, when they don't know the least thing about it.

RUDDLE (*rising and going down R.*). Hear ! hear !

(*She gives him a hasty glance, but the entrance of CICELY saves the situation. She carries a tray holding a jug of milk and several glasses. During the next few speeches, CICELY pours out the milk and hands the glasses round When she has completed this task she exits unobtrusively.*)

PRUDENCE (*who has propped up the paper in front of her and is reading as she eats*). Dear me!

TILDA. Anything in the paper, Prudence ?

PRUDENCE. Of course there's something in the paper ! How could they sell it, otherwise ?

TILDA (*meekly*). I meant anything of interest, dear.

PRUDENCE. There's something very peculiar here. Listen to this: " New disease threatens to sweep the country. Malayan Measles Scare ! "

TILDA. Malaya—where's that ?

PRUDENCE. Don't be so ignorant, Tilda. Everyone knows where Malaya is. It's—it's——

FAITH. Yes, Aunt ?

PRUDENCE. It's—it's somewhere out East, of course !

TILDA. Oh !

FAITH. What does it say about it, Aunt ?

PRUDENCE. I was trying to tell you—(*Glaring at TILDA*)—before I was interrupted.

TILDA. I'm sorry, dear. Please go on.

PRUDENCE. Very well. Listen: " Grave concern

is being felt in this country owing to the spread of an unknown infectious disease, which, though fairly mild in character, is particularly unpleasant for the sufferer.   After an incubation period of about a fortnight, a rash develops, followed by a violent itching ; and wholesale inoculations are being carried out in an effort to prevent further spreading.   The germs, which in many respects closely resemble those of the common childhood complaint of measles, have been isolated by a Malayan doctor now resident in this country ; and for want of a better name scientists are labelling the new disease —Malayan Measles ! "

BOB. Malayan Measles ? That's a funny name.

RUDDLE. Lot o' rubbish, 'tis.   Fancy coming home from the " Foresters' Arms " some night and being told as you've got Hungarian Hiccups !

PRUDENCE (*sternly*). No one asked for your observations, Ruddle !

(*A hostile glance passes between them.*)

FAITH (*who with* BOB *has opened the window curtains, and is looking out*). Oh, Mother ! There's a lovely new moon.

PRUDENCE. New moon ? Then I must turn my money over.   (*She produces a purse from her pocket and opens it.*)

BOB. Really, Ma'am. I didn't know you were superstitious ?

PRUDENCE. Superstitious ? Young man, if you'd been brought up in a household like I was, you'd be superstitious !   Why, every time a thunderstorm came on, my mother even used to cover up the sewing-machine !

RUDDLE. Some o' the folks in the village does that yet.

PRUDENCE. What—when it lightens ?

RUDDLE. No. When the man calls for the instalments.

PRUDENCE. The man's a fool. Mr. Sladen, won't

you sit down?   (*Indicating vacant chair R. of table.*)

BOB.   Thanks, no.   I'll stand with Ned, if you don't mind.   (*He crosses R.*)

PRUDENCE.   As you please.   Faith!   Hand the biscuits round.

(FAITH *takes plates to* BOB *and* NED.   TILDA *follows* PRUDENCE'S *example and helps herself at the table.*)

RUDDLE   (*thoughtfully*).   It's mighty funny, though!

PRUDENCE.   What is?

RUDDLE.   You being superstitious.

PRUDENCE.   Why, pray?

RUDDLE.   Because o' this house.

PRUDENCE.   What on earth do you mean?

RUDDLE.   Well, if ever superstition were proved to be correct, this here farm is a shining example. It's rather a long story, though.

FAITH.   Oh, Ned!   Do tell us!

RUDDLE.   Not me!   I'm always being told about speaking out o' my turn.

PRUDENCE.   Come on, Ruddle.   Don't beat about the bush!   Perhaps this'll be about the first time the man has had something really interesting to say.

RUDDLE.   On second thoughts, I'd better not!   I don't want to upset the Missus.

TILDA.   Upset me?

PRUDENCE.   Get on with it, Ruddle!   Do as you're told.

RUDDLE.   Very well—but you've brought it on yourselves, remember!   (*He takes a long pull at the milk, then continues.*)   Well, it were this way.   I've been at this place a tidy long while now.   Let me see—it'll be——

FAITH.   Forty years, Ned?

RUDDLE.   Forty-one!   Howsomever, that's beside the point.   When I first came here, this place was owned by old Mr. Grantham. A queer old fish, he was,—and his wife, too !

PRUDENCE (*impatiently*).   Well, where does the superstition come in ?

RUDDLE.   I'm coming to that.   I remembers it perfectly—in fact, I shall never forget it.   Both of their pictures used to hang up on that wall!' (*He points to the back wall.*)

PRUDENCE.   Well ?

RUDDLE.   Well, one night, they was setting round all nice and quiet, when suddenly there was a terrific crash, and one o' those pictures came tumbling to the ground.   It was the old lady's !   The cord must have snapped, and the glass was smashed to atoms.

PRUDENCE.   Yes, but I don't see——

RUDDLE.   Don't you ?   Then listen to this ! (*Dramatically.*)   A week later the old lady was carried out o' the house for the last time !   I was one o' the bearers !

TILDA.   Mercy on us !

PRUDENCE.   Don't be silly, Tilda.   A mere co-incidence !   Nothing more.

RUDDLE.   Then how do you account for this ? Two years later, the old man's picture crashed down the same, and in less than a week he was lying alongside her !

PRUDENCE (*more impressed*).   Hm !   That would appear to be a very remarkable coincidence.

RUDDLE.   Aye—and that's not all!

PRUDENCE.   Not all ?

RUDDLE.   Not by some !   Several years later, their son—young Mr. Grantham—he lived along of 'em as well—he had the very same experience !

PRUDENCE (*aghast*).   Never !

RUDDLE.   He did !

TILDA.   And did he die too ?

RUDDLE.   No.   You see, he knew what had happened before, and he thought it might be a curse or something as hung over the place.   So he sold the farm to the Master—(*To* PRUDENCE)—your brother—and cleared out the very next day.

TILDA. Then he's still living?

RUDDLE. As far as I know.   At least he were twelve months ago.

PRUDENCE. Then doesn't that disprove the theory of the—er—pictures?

RUDDLE. It might have done—but there was something else!

TILDA. Something else?

RUDDLE. Yes—though I don't think I ought to mention it—not now.

PRUDENCE. Of course you will!   You can't leave a story half-finished like that.

RUDDLE. Well, I don't like to, really.   Still I don't suppose it matters now—it's too late to do anything about it!

PRUDENCE. Go on!

RUDDLE. Well, a week before the Master died——

PRUDENCE. Yes?

RUDDLE. That there picture of him (*pointing to picture above fireplace*) tumbled down just the very same!

TILDA. WHAT? (*She becomes very perturbed.*) Oh dear!   Oh dear!   Why didn't you tell me? I knew nothing about it!

RUDDLE. I didn't want to alarm you.   Luckily the glass wasn't broken, so I fastened on some new cord, and put it back before anyone found out.

PRUDENCE. But didn't you warn my brother?

RUDDLE. Naturally.   I begged him, implored him, to go away and save himself, same as young Mr. Grantham. (*Shaking his head sadly.*)   But he was always stubborn, was the Master!

(*There is stunned silence for a moment.*   NED *winks broadly at* BOB.   BOB, *for the first time realising the game, barely represses a laugh, and takes* FAITH *over to the back to enlighten her.*)

TILDA (*very much moved*).   Oh dear!   And to

think poor Tom might still have been with us to-day !

PRUDENCE (*staggered*). Remarkable ! Most remarkable ! I can hardly believe it possible. And yet, it all goes to prove, Tilda, that stranger things are happening all around us than we could ever imagine in our wildest dreams.

RUDDLE. Well, you asked for the story—and you've got it, though I'm sorry now as I ever mentioned it. I fully intended to keep it locked in my bosom till I carried it to the grave.

PRUDENCE (*graciously*). That's all right, Ruddle. You've done the right thing, however painful it may have been. The knowledge of this may be a very vital thing some day. Who knows ?

RUDDLE. Ah, who knows ? (*Placing glass on table.*) Well, I'll be turning in. That rehearsing's knocked me over—and a good night's rest'll happen cheer us up a bit. (*He moves up the stairs.*) Good-night, all !

FAITH ⎫
BOB ⎬ (*together*). Good-night, Ned !

PRUDENCE. Good-night, Ruddle.

(RUDDLE *disappears through the curtains.*)

BOB. Well, I suppose I'd better be getting along too.

FAITH. I'll see you to the gate, Mr. Sladen.

PRUDENCE. Is that absolutely necessary ?

FAITH. Yes, Aunt. There are several things lying about out there, and in the dark it's so easy to trip over something.

PRUDENCE. In the dark ? Then that new moon has disappeared very quickly !

TILDA. It's the trees, Prudence. They make the place awfully shady, even in the day-time.

PRUDENCE. Oh, very well. Off you go ! But don't be long !

FAITH. No, Aunt.

BOB (*at door, back*). Good-night, Mrs. Hannacott ! Good-night, Ma'am !

PRUDENCE. Good-night, young man.   And remember—the evenings are chilly, so don't stand
talking !

BOB. I'll remember.

(*He exits, allowing* FAITH *to precede him.*)

TILDA (*after a slight pause*).   Rather a nice young
man. don't you think?

PRUDENCE. Who ?

TILDA. Bob Sladen.

PRUDENCE. They all are—till you get to know
them !

(*Slight pause.*)

TILDA. Prudence.

PRUDENCE. Yes ?

TILDA. I can't help thinking about—about Ned
Ruddle !

PRUDENCE. What he was saying ?

TILDA. Yes.

PRUDENCE. It was rather staggering, wasn't it ?

TILDA. If only Tom had told me.   I'm sure I
might have persuaded him to—to——

PRUDENCE. Leave ?

TILDA. Yes.

PRUDENCE. Ah well !   It's too late to think of
that now.   Time enough when it happens again.

TILDA (*alarmed*). Oh, Prudence !   Do you think
it might ?

PRUDENCE. No !   If it's happened four times in
the last forty years, we can safely say that it will
never happen again.

TILDA. Never ?

PRUDENCE. Well, not in our generation !

(*Suddenly there is a bang, and the picture above the
stairs crashes to the ground.   Both women jump
up and turn to look.   PRUDENCE emits a loud
scream, and collapses back in her seat.*)

PRUDENCE. Water !   WATER !

TILDA. Help ! Help ! Ned ! Faith ! Water !
Fetch some water !

(CICELY *appears at the door R., then* BOB *and* FAITH
*enter hurriedly at the back door. They all rush
over. Next* RUDDLE *appears at the top of the
stairs. He is dressed in a long nightgown, and
carries the jug from a wash-hand basin. They
all crowd round* PRUDENCE, *who has fainted
away.* RUDDLE *clumsily attempts to give her a
drink from the jug.*)

BOB. What's the matter, Mrs. Hannacott ?

TILDA (*almost beside herself*). Aunt Prudence !
That picture !

RUDDLE. It fell, did it ?

TILDA. Just like you've been saying—and then
she screamed !

RUDDLE. No wonder. That picture's hers !

TILDA (*terrified*). Hers ?

RUDDLE. Aye. I hung it for her—Saturday
morning.

TILDA. Oh, dear ! Whatever shall we do ?

(RUDDLE *crosses and picks up the picture. Making
sure that he is not observed by the others, he
surreptitiously cuts the cord with a knife.*)

BOB (*who has been attending to* PRUDENCE). Wait
a minute! She's coming round, I think. (*To*
PRUDENCE.) There, Ma'am ! That's better now !
Take it easy. That's the way.

PRUDENCE (*coming to*). Oh ! I—I—(*Looking
round at all of them.*) What happened ?

RUDDLE. Your picture—it fell.

CICELY. Fa-ancy tha-at !

PRUDENCE. Oh, yes. I remember ! Oh, Tilda
dear, whatever are we going to do ?

RUDDLE. Best be guided by young Mr. Grantham
The sooner you leaves the better !

PRUDENCE. The sooner *I* leave ?

FAITH. Of course !

PRUDENCE. But why should I leave ?

RUDDLE. Well, if it's your picture——!

PRUDENCE. But it isn't !

RUDDLE. WHAT ! !

PRUDENCE. It isn't !

RUDDLE (aghast). But you told me it was yours !

PRUDENCE. So I did ! It was given to me twenty-five years ago by my dear Brother. But the photograph isn't mine !

RUDDLE. Holy smoke !

FAITH. Then whose is it ?

PRUDENCE. It's your Mother's.

RUDDLE ⎫
FAITH ⎬ (together). WHAT ! ! !
BOB   ⎭

PRUDENCE. It's your dear Mother's—TAKEN ON HER TWENTY-FIRST BIRTHDAY !

[TILDA snatches the picture from RUDDLE, takes one look at it, screams, and collapses in a faint. The others catch her and help her to a chair. RUDDLE waves the picture frantically before her face, as : —

the CURTAIN falls.

ACT III.

SCENE: *The Living-room of the Hannacott Farm-house, as before.*
TIME: *The following afternoon.*

The curtain rises on the same setting as in ACT I and ACT II. It is the afternoon of the day following the picture disaster. The lamp has now disappeared. The window-curtains are open, revealing a bright, sunny day outside. The curtains across the stairs are similarly open.

CICELY *is discovered, evidently clearing the table after the mid-day meal. She is piling dirty crockery on her tray, and removing the white cloth. She is singing to herself in an absent-minded sort of way.*

Almost immediately FAITH *enters down the stairs, also carrying a tray of pots, evidently the remains of a meal which has been served upstairs.*

FAITH (*going back and depositing tray on dresser*). Singing, Cicely?

CICELY (*clapping hand to mouth*). Oh, I beg your pardon, Miss, I'm sure! I'd clean forgotten myself. How is the Missus now?

FAITH. Ever so much better, thanks. Since I had a little chat with her this morning, she's brightened up considerably.

CICELY. Fa-ancy tha-at! (*Also taking tray to dresser.*) It's funny how the Missus always catches it. Nothing seems to upset t'other one!

FAITH. Aunt Prudence, you mean?

CICELY. Yes, Miss.

FAITH. She's pretty hardy, isn't she?

CICELY. Hardy? (*Coming back to table and dusting off crumbs.*) If Old Nick were suddenly to

71

appear before her, she'd tell him to go round to the tradesman's entrance !

FAITH (*laughing*). You'd better tell that to Ned Ruddle.

CICELY. I will, Miss ! By the way—have you heard the news ?

FAITH. No.

CICELY. It's all over the village. Young Peter Yorke has been taken away !

FAITH. Taken away ? What for ?

CICELY. The doctor didn't seem rightly to know. They rushed him off to the fever hospital and called in a specialist. He suspects it's this new-fangled thing that there's been so much about in the papers just lately.

FAITH. Do you mean Malayan Measles ?

CICELY. That's it !

FAITH. Good gracious ! We shall have to be careful then, shan't we ?

CICELY. Oh, and that reminds me ! I knew there was something else. (*Looking around.*) Miss Faith, would you mind if I was to speak confidential-like ?

FAITH (*coming down and sitting R. of table*). Not at all. What is it ?

CICELY (*coming closer to her after making sure door R. is closed*). Something strange has happened to me. I've started thinking !

FAITH (*smiling*). Is that *very* strange, Cicely ?

CICELY (*now on FAITH's R.*). No, Miss, you don't understand. It's about Ned Ruddle. I've been wondering if he had anything to do with that picture business last night.

FAITH. What makes you think that ?

CICELY (*dipping hand into pocket, and displaying something*). This !

FAITH. What is it ?

CICELY. Half-a-crown.

FAITH. Oh, the half-crown he owed you. He's paid it, then ?

CICELY. Yes, Miss.

FAITH. But I don't see the connection between that and—— ?

CICELY. The picture ?

(FAITH *nods*.)

Well, I'll tell you. I'd been thinking it over this morning, and I began to feel as Ned might be at the bottom of last night's affair, especially after the other business. So while he was having his breakfast here, I taxed him with it.

FAITH. And what happened ?

CICELY. Well, I expected him to go up in a blue light, but he didn't do nothing of the sort. He sat and stared at me for fully a minute, then he dipped his hand in his pocket and gave me this.

FAITH. And what did you do ?

CICELY. I asked him if he'd paid just to sweeten me.

FAITH. Sweeten you ?

CICELY. To keep my mouth closed ! I got that out o' the " Film Weekly."

FAITH. I see. And what did he say ?

CICELY (*moving C. behind table*). Something as I didn't rightly understand—but it frightened me all the same.

FAITH. What was it ?

CICELY (*sitting behind table*). He said : " Cicely, I've paid you now ! Your blood be on your own head ! " I asked him what he meant. He says : "As long as I didn't pay you, you were innocent in the eyes o' the law ; but now you've taken money for it, you're just as guilty as I am. And if the Police ever gets to know what you did wi' that tea-pot—they'll take you as an un-necessary both afore and after the fact ! "

FAITH. I think I understand what he meant.

CICELY (*anxiously*). Then can he do it, Miss ?

FAITH. Yes, I'm afraid he can. But I don't think he would.

CICELY. No, he said he wouldn't—on condition I promised never to repeat to anybody else in this house what I'd hinted about that picture.

FAITH. And you promised?

CICELY. Yes. I thought it best.

FAITH. Then you've soon broken it, haven't you?

(CICELY *rises*.)

CICELY (*puzzled*). But I've never said a word!

FAITH. You have!

CICELY. When?

FAITH. To me. Just now!

CICELY (*alarmed*). Oh, Miss Faith. I didn't mean to, really I didn't! You won't tell on me, will you?

FAITH (*rising*). No, I won't. But you'd better be more careful in future. If ever I catch you saying it to anyone else—Aunt Prudence, for example— I might be tempted to tell Ned Ruddle all about it.

CICELY. Trust me, Miss. (*Licking her finger and drawing it across her throat.*) See that wet—see that dry! I'll never breathe a word to a soul, honest I won't! Least of all *her*! If I tried to tell her anything, I'm sure my tongue would go back on me.

(NED RUDDLE *and* BOB SLADEN *both pass across behind the window towards the back door.*)

FAITH. Very well. Oh, here's Ned now!

CICELY. Lor'!

FAITH. You'd better get on with the washing-up, in case he asks any awkward questions.

CICELY. Yes, Miss.

(CICELY *seizes one tray of crockery, and disappears through the door R. as the back door opens, and* BOB *and* RUDDLE *enter.*)

BOB (*entering first*). Hello, Faith!

FAITH (*coldly*). Well, Mr. Sladen! (*Resting

against front of table.)   To what do we owe the honour of this visit ?   A sympathy call—or another shareholders' meeting of Conspirators Limited ?

Bob (*down R.*).   I'm terribly sorry, Faith !   I had no hand in it.   (*Pointing to* Ruddle, *who has crossed L. at the back, and is standing staring gloomily into the empty fireplace.*)   It was all *his* doing.   You know that !

Ruddle (*without looking up*).   Aye—blame me ! If it had come off, you'd have been taking all the credit, I suppose ?

Faith (*turning on him*).   Well, it was your fault, wasn't it ?   It was *your* grand idea !

Ruddle (*turning to her*).   If anyone were to blame —it were you !   (*Pointing at her.*)

Faith (*warmly*).   Me ?   How do you make that out ?

Ruddle (*turning back to fire*).   Even a calf knows its own Mother !

Faith.   And I should have recognised mine on that photograph, I suppose ?

Ruddle.   Aye !

Faith (*going L. towards* Ruddle).   Well, let me tell you, Ned Ruddle, it was too small to be seen properly up there.   If you'd shown it to me before you put it up, I might have had a chance to recognise it !

Ruddle.   There you go again !   I knew it'd work back to me.   It always does !

Bob.   How's your Mother, Faith ?

Faith (*returning R.C. towards* Bob).   She was in a dreadful state this morning !

Bob.   She might well be.

Faith.   But she's ever so much better now—since I told her the whole story.

Ruddle (*astounded*).   You did what ?

Faith.   Told her the whole story !   The truth about how the picture did come down.

Ruddle.   Crikey !

Bob.   That was a bit risky, wasn't it ?

FAITH. Risky or not, it had to be done ! Don't you see, Bob, poor Mother would have worried herself to death if I hadn't made a clean breast of it.

BOB. Then you told her Ned's story was nothing but a—— ?

FAITH. Pack of lies ? Yes !

RUDDLE. That's what you say now. Last night you thought it was brilliant.

BOB (*grudgingly*). Well—you did make it rather convincing, Ned.

RUDDLE (*indignantly*). Convincing ? Afore I'd finished, I were ready to believe in it myself !

BOB (*to* FAITH). And how did your Mother take it ?

FAITH. Very badly at first. But when I explained that it was all done for Aunt Prudence's benefit, she was more inclined to see reason.

BOB. Then she won't split ?

FAITH. To Aunt Prudence ? No, I don't think so.

RUDDLE. You didn't by any chance inform her about the tea-party as well ?

FAITH. No. I thought that was best forgotten.

RUDDLE (*with a sigh of relief*). Thank the Lord for that !

BOB. What about your Aunt—how's she ?

FAITH. Just the same. As firmly fixed as ever.

RUDDLE. Like the rock o' Gibraltar — only stonier !

FAITH. She's tried to persuade Mother to pack up and go away for a few weeks.

BOB. And will she go ?

FAITH. Not now—now that she knows the truth.

BOB. Everything seems to be pretty much " as you were," then ?

RUDDLE. Aye—and the sergeant-major's still in command. But we'll soon alter that !

BOB. How ?

RUDDLE (*moving C. towards the others*). Well, I've been thinking. I've got an idea as'll——

FAITH. Oh, no, you don't !

RUDDLE. What?

FAITH. I say—no, you don't. Your ideas are so clever that they always go astray. Why, you've even scared poor Cicely now with some cock and bull story about the Police !

RUDDLE (*sadly*). Aye—I seem to be able to scare anybody in this house—only the right 'un ! (*Brightening up.*) But wait till you've heard this one ! This is a snorter !

FAITH. We're not going to hear it. We've finished !

RUDDLE (*horrified*). But surely, Miss, you're not going to give in already ? Admit defeat so soon ? Not likely !

FAITH (*firmly*). I said we've finished—and I mean it !

RUDDLE. What—and take our medicine lying down ! Daily doses of it for six years ! Oh, Missy, have a heart ! Let's have one more try ! It's the last straw that breaks the camel's back, you know. Just one more chance, and if that goes west—— !

FAITH. Very well. You shall have another chance.

RUDDLE. Hurrah !

FAITH. On one condition !

RUDDLE. What's that ?

FAITH. That somebody else thinks of the idea !

RUDDLE. Here ! But that's not fair !

FAITH. Why not ?

RUDDLE. Seems mighty-like to me as though you're trying to diddle me out of that pound.

BOB. No. she's not, Ned. Remember what I said : " On the day she leaves this house for good— it'll be worth a pound note in your pocket."

(*The door R. opens suddenly.*)

FAITH (*putting her finger to her lips*). Sh !

(CICELY *enters rather nervously. She approaches the dresser for the second tray of crockery, her*

eyes fixed on RUDDLE *the whole time.* RUDDLE
*sticks his thumbs in the armholes of his waist-
coat, and stares at her fiercely. Just as she gets
her hands on the tray he gives a sudden throaty
cough.* CICELY *grabs the tray and flies back
through the door like a startled rabbit.)*

FAITH (*laughing*). Poor Cicely !

RUDDLE (*relaxing*). Aye. Well, to get back to
business. That seems fair enough to me. Who's
going to give us the idea ?

FAITH. Oh, Bob or I, I suppose.

RUDDLE. Well, come on, then—spill it.   And if
it's any worse than mine—— !

FAITH. It couldn't be !

BOB. Ladies first. What do you suggest, Faith ?

FAITH (*resting against front of table*). I haven't
the slightest idea.

RUDDLE. That's helpful !   (*To* BOB.) What about
you ?

BOB. Well—I haven't really considered it.

RUDDLE (*to* FAITH). There you are, see !   Now
my idea is this. If we were to—— (*Sitting L. of
table.*)

BOB (*suddenly, and going down R.*). Wait a
minute ! It might—— Yes, it might possibly——

RUDDLE. What's the matter ? Thought o' something ?

BOB. Just a rough idea—that's all.

RUDDLE. Well, don't waste time ! Let's hear it.

BOB. You've been down to the village this morning, haven't you ?

RUDDLE. Certainly.   To the station over those
blessed milk-cans.

BOB. Then you've heard about young Peter
Yorke ?

RUDDLE. Aye—'tis all over the village. Malayan
Measles, they reckon !

BOB. Yes. I was thinking perhaps that might
help us.

RUDDLE. How ?

BOB.   Malayan Measles might be a very dangerous
thing.   It might be dangerous enough to frighten
Miss Hannacott away.

RUDDLE. Rubbish !   Take more than that to
scare her away.   Besides, there is no danger really.

BOB.   No, but there might be.

RUDDLE. How ?

BOB.   Well, supposing some of the germs were to
find their way into this house ?

RUDDLE. Ridic'lous !   There's not the slightest
chance.

BOB. Isn't there ?   That's just where you're
wrong.

RUDDLE. But how could they ?

BOB.   Well, if someone in this house were to
catch this Malayan Measles——

RUDDLE. There's nobody likely to do that !

BOB.   Oh yes, there is.

RUDDLE. Who ?

BOB.   You !

RUDDLE. WHAT ?

BOB.   You !

RUDDLE. ME ?

BOB.   Yes !

RUDDLE (*rising*).   Don't be daft !

BOB.   There's nothing daft about it.   Someone's
going to catch Malayan Measles in this house—and
that someone's going to be—*you* !

RUDDLE. Listen, Bob Sladen !   If you think I'm
going to hang round young Peter Yorke's neck for
your sake, you're mightily mistaken.

BOB.   It's not for my sake.   It's the best way of
getting rid of her.

RUDDLE. Aye, it's the best way o' getting rid o'
me, too !

FAITH.   Don't be silly, Ned.   I can see Bob's idea.
You're not going to get it really.

RUDDLE (*grimly*).   You're   right.   I'm   not !
(*Going back.*)

BOB. Don't you see, Ned? All you've got to do is *pretend* that you've got Malayan Measles.

RUDDLE. Eh?

BOB. I say, you only pretend to have it.

RUDDLE (*reassured*). Oh well, that's different! But wouldn't it be better if you had it? (*Coming R.C. behind table.*)

BOB. Why?

RUDDLE (*vaguely*). Well, you know more about what it's like, maybe.

BOB. No, it's got to be *you*!

RUDDLE. Why?

BOB. Because—well—you want to earn that pound, don't you?

RUDDLE. Yes, please.

BOB. Then this is your chance. (*Taking* RUDDLE *by the arm.*) Now you come along with me and I'll explain to you exactly what I want you to do.

TILDA (*off*). Faith! Faith!

FAITH. Look out! That's Mother.

RUDDLE. I thought she was in bed!

FAITH. No, she's getting up. She was dressing when I left her. You'd better clear out before she comes down.

RUDDLE. Aye, she may have a few things to say to me.

FAITH. She most certainly has.

RUDDLE. Then I'm off! Come on, Bob.

(*They exit through the back door.* FAITH *crosses to the window and stands looking out.* TILDA *enters via the stairs, book in hand.*)

TILDA. Ah, there you are, Faith. Who was that just went out? Ned Ruddle?

FAITH. Yes, Mother.

TILDA. I thought it was. Could tell his voice. It's a good job he has gone, too! I'll give him a piece of my mind, that I will. Him and his monkey-tricks!

FAITH (*crossing to* TILDA *and helping her to the*

rocking-chair). Now, Mother, you mustn't be angry with him. He didn't mean any harm.

TILDA. Didn't mean it? Perhaps he didn't, but he's caused enough.

FAITH. Now you mustn't excite yourself, you know. Just try and forget all about it !

TILDA. Forget all about it ? How can I, when all the time I'm afraid there's something else going on behind my back ?

FAITH. Have you heard about Peter Yorke ? They believe he's got this new Measles disease !

TILDA. Yes. Your Aunt's told me all about it. (*Sharply.*) And don't try to change the conversation.

FAITH (*with a sigh*). Yes, Mother.

TILDA. I was talking about Ned Ruddle. Now, Faith, I want you to understand, once and for all, that nothing like this must happen again.

FAITH. Very well.

TILDA. And what's more, I absolutely insist that no more of these tricks shall be played upon your Aunt, unless——

FAITH. Unless what ?

TILDA. Unless I'm told about it beforehand !

FAITH (*slipping her arms around* TILDA'S *neck*). I see. Then you're not really angry ?

TILDA (*also smiling*). Not really. (*Hardening again.*) Though I've every right to be !

FAITH. Of course you have, dear. Anyway, let's forget about it now. (*Picking up book from* TILDA'S *lap.*) What's this ? "Age Shall Not Wither." Going to learn some of your part ?

TILDA. I've been trying to—but I find it awfully difficult.

FAITH. Then I'll help you. (*Dragging chair from L. of table to side of rocking-chair.*) I'll read the speeches in between.

TILDA. Very well, dear.

FAITH. Let me see. Who are you ?

TILDA. Miss Berryman—Prudence Berryman.

FAITH. Prudence ? I say, that's funny. Just like Auntie !

TILDA. Yes, and goodness knows it's confusing enough without that.

FAITH. Never mind. We'll begin here—where Cornelius enters. He says first: "Sit down."

TILDA. And I reply: "I beg your pardon ? "

FAITH. Good ! Then he repeats it: "Sit down !"

TILDA (*bothered*). Dear me ! I'm afraid I've for-gotten. Is it me now ?

FAITH. No, not yet. He says: "Prudence,—I may call you Prudence, I suppose ? "

TILDA. "Certainly—if you wish ! " That's right, isn't it ?

FAITH. Yes, Mother. Then he says: "Ever since you——"

(*The door, back, opens, and* PRUDENCE *enters.*)

PRUDENCE. Hello—what's going on now ?

FAITH. I was just helping Mother to go through her part.

PRUDENCE (*removing hat, and hanging it on one of the pegs above the stairs*). You would be ! Nothing else to do, I suppose, in a busy place like this ?

TILDA. Put it away, dear. We'll finish it some other time.

(FAITH *closes the book, rises, and crosses to the dresser, putting the book away in a drawer.*)

FAITH. Been out, Aunt ?

PRUDENCE (*snappishly*). Of course I've been out ! What a foolish question ! Do you think I put my hat on to go to bed ?

TILDA. Have you been far ?

PRUDENCE. As far as the station—that's all.

FAITH. Those milk-cans again ?

PRUDENCE. Yes. I sent Ruddle this morning. When he came back I asked him if the cans were at the station, and he said: "No, they're not ! "

FAITH. So you went to put it right?

PRUDENCE (*sitting R. of table*). Well, I gave them a nice quiet word of advice!

TILDA. What was that?

PRUDENCE. I told them if those cans weren't back here first thing in the morning, I'd sue them!

TILDA. Good gracious! And what did the station-master say to that?

PRUDENCE. Laughed in my face!

TILDA. Never!

PRUDENCE. Yes, he did. Laughed in my face, and told me to get on with the suing!

TILDA. Whatever for?

PRUDENCE (*with a nasty glance*). Because he'd given them to Ned Ruddle to bring home this morning!

TILDA. Then you haven't seen Ned yet?

PRUDENCE. Not yet. But just wait till I do!

FAITH. Poor Ned! He's in trouble all round.

PRUDENCE (*sharply*). What's that?

FAITH. Oh, nothing, Aunt. Nothing at all.

PRUDENCE. Well, Tilda, you're up?

FAITH (*slyly*). What a foolish question, Aunt Prudence. She doesn't put her clothes on and come downstairs to go to bed, does she?

PRUDENCE. Don't be impertinent, child!

FAITH. But you said a few minutes ago——

PRUDENCE. I don't need to be reminded of what I said. When you asked if I had been out, it *was* a most foolish question, because it was obvious that I had been out. But in this case it wasn't obvious that—er—— (*realising she is in difficulties*).

FAITH (*still slyly*). That Mother was up? No—perhaps it wasn't.

PRUDENCE. That's quite enough! We'll consider that closed. (*Crossing and sitting in chair where* FAITH *had been previously.*) Now, Tilda, how are you feeling?

TILDA. Much better, thanks.

PRUDENCE. And you are still determined after what has happened, not to go away?

TILDA. Quite determined.

PRUDENCE. Then you're a very foolish woman, Tilda.

TILDA. Maybe I am.

PRUDENCE. Now, if it had been me.

FAITH. Ah! If! (*She sighs.*)

PRUDENCE (*after a reproving glance*). I say, if it had been me——

FAITH. You'd have gone away, wouldn't you, Aunt?

PRUDENCE. Most certainly!

TILDA (*unthinkingly*). What a pity!

PRUDENCE. Tilda!

TILDA. I mean it's a pity that you should feel that way about it. I don't—not now.

PRUDENCE. Then you won't go?

TILDA. No. I'll see it through.

PRUDENCE. Ah, well; it's your own funeral.

TILDA (*shocked*). Prudence!

FAITH. Yes, Aunt. That wasn't a very nice remark!

PRUDENCE. I'm sorry. It was a little drastic—but quite unintentional. The kind of remark one would expect from Ruddle!

(MISS LOVEDAY *crosses past outside the window.*)

FAITH (*observing her*). Here comes Miss Loveday.

PRUDENCE. What, again! The woman will be living here shortly.

(*There comes a tap at the door, then it opens and* MISS LOVEDAY *enters.*)

LOVEDAY. Hello, everyone. May I come inside?

FAITH (*laughing*). Another obvious one, Aunt?

LOVEDAY. I don't quite understand. Have I made a "faux pas"?

PRUDENCE. Not at all. Miss Loveday. Seeing that you *are* inside, you may as well close the door.

LOVEDAY (*complying*). Oh, certainly! Certainly!

PRUDENCE. Are you not at school to-day?

(FAITH *laughs*.)

(*Haughtily*.) What I meant was—how is it that you are not at school?

LOVEDAY. It's a half-holiday. We had the Scripture Examiners this morning.

PRUDENCE (*sarcastically*). I see. I suppose the little darlings were quite thrilled?

LOVEDAY. Oh, they weren't little. One was a big, fat gentleman with glasses; and the other——

PRUDENCE (*coldly*). I meant the children.

LOVEDAY. The children? (*Comprehending*.) Oh yes, they were quite excited! Not about the examination, of course.

PRUDENCE. Naturally! (*Coldly*.) Well, you mustn't waste your half-holiday, must you?

LOVEDAY (*ignorant of the implication*). Oh, I'm not wasting it! I should have come over to see you in any case.

PRUDENCE. What I meant was that as you are not compelled to work this afternoon—*as we are*—you would possibly find it more congenial out in the open air!

LOVEDAY (*still unsuspecting*). Ah, yes. It would be pleasanter out in the garden; but we can talk in here just as well, can't we, dear?

PRUDENCE. Miss Loveday, will you—— !

LOVEDAY (*wagging a finger at her*). No, no! I mustn't stop! (*She settles herself in the chair R. of table*.) I know you must be terribly busy, but I'm not the kind of person to outstay my welcome. Oh dear no!

PRUDENCE. Really?

LOVEDAY. Yes. But that's the trouble with most

people like yourself. They're far too polite to tell you that they are busy.

PRUDENCE. Indeed ! I wasn't aware of it.

LOVEDAY. Ah, dear Miss Hannacott, you're too modest—far too modest !

FAITH (*slyly*). I don't suppose you were aware of that either, Aunt ?

(PRUDENCE *gives her a sharp look, but* MISS LOVE-DAY *prattles on gaily.*)

LOVEDAY. Of course, I wouldn't have bothered you at all, if it hadn't been frightfully important. Now let me see—what was it that I came to see you about ? (*Slight pause.*) Ah yes,—— (*Slight pause.*) No ! (*Slight pause, then a foolish sort of laugh.*) Dear, dear ! Silly of me, isn't it ? I'm afraid I've forgotten what it was, just for the moment.

PRUDENCE. It must have been *frightfully* important !

LOVEDAY. Oh, it was ! (*Racking her brain.*) Dear me ! This fickle thing called memory ! It makes one look so stupid, don't you think ?

PRUDENCE. The memory is not entirely responsible in some cases, Miss Loveday !

LOVEDAY. Ah, well—perhaps it will come back to me in a minute or two.

PRUDENCE. If it doesn't—it may be too late !

LOVEDAY. Oh dear no ! Never too late ! If I should have to go before I remember—I say if I *should* have to go—I can always slip back again.

PRUDENCE. That will be quite unnecessary.

LOVEDAY. No trouble, Miss Hannacott. No trouble, I assure you ! (*Suddenly thinking.*) Trouble ? Wait a moment ! That reminds me ! Trouble ? (*Excitedly.*) Ah, yes, I've got it ! I remember now !

PRUDENCE. Well ?

LOVEDAY (*her face clouding over again*). No, I'm afraid not ! That was the other thing.

PRUDENCE (*exasperated*). Suppose we hear " the other thing," before you forget that ?

LOVEDAY. To be sure ! It was the word " trouble " that reminded me. You know the little bit of trouble that took place here last night ? (*Triumphantly.*) Well, I've got to the bottom of it !

FAITH (*involuntarily*). The picture ? (*She puts her hand to her mouth almost as soon as she realises the slip.*)

LOVEDAY. Did I say " picture " ? Good gracious me ! What has come over me ! I can't even re- member what I'm saying now.

PRUDENCE. Please continue, Miss Loveday.

LOVEDAY. It's the dear Colonel's wife. I went round to see her this morning before school, and she was penitent—most penitent ! She even con- fessed that she'd never read the play through.

PRUDENCE. That was perfectly obvious !

LOVEDAY. However, she begged me to release her from the part, so I've changed her over with Mrs. Crabtree and put her in the third play. Mrs. Crab- tree will now play Mrs. Fotheringay.

TILDA. Well, that settles that.

LOVEDAY. Not quite ! The Colonel's wife feels that she still owes you an apology for her be- haviour——

PRUDENCE. And she's sent you round to deliver it ?

LOVEDAY. Dear me, no ! Nothing of the sort. She said that she would call round this afternoon and deliver it in person.

PRUDENCE. How delightful ! (*Firmly, and ris- ing.*) Well, I'm sorry you must be going, Miss Love- day.

LOVEDAY. Must I ? Ah yes, of course ; you're busy, aren't you ? (*Rising.*) I quite understand (*Crossing to back door.*) And with regard to the other matter—it will probably come to me quite suddenly—quite suddenly—and if so——

PRUDENCE. Yes, yes, we understand. Good-bye, Miss Loveday !

LOVEDAY. Good-bye, and thank you so much !

FAITH
TILDA } (*together*). Good-bye !

(MISS LOVEDAY *goes out, leaving the door ajar. She has only just crossed the threshold, however, when she suddenly swings round, and rushes back to the door.*)

LOVEDAY (*excitedly*). Wait a moment ! I believe I—— ! (*Slight pause.*) No ! (*Shaking her head sadly.*) No, it's no use ! (*Smiling and wagging her finger at them, while she pulls the door behind her with the other hand.*) Ah, well. It'll come ! All in good time ! Yes, it'll be sure to come ! Good-bye ! Good-bye !

(*She closes the door, and a moment later passes across L. outside the window.*)

PRUDENCE. And there goes the fountain of knowledge from which the young minds of this village sip divine wisdom !

TILDA. She isn't so bad, Prudence, when you get to know her properly.

PRUDENCE (*sitting again*). Well, if that's a fair sample of her powers of memorisation, all I can say is that it's a good job she didn't sit for her own Scripture Examination ! Now if *I* had something frightfully important to tell someone, I——

TILDA. By the way, Prudence. Did you remind Cicely about getting that order off for the cream ?

PRUDENCE. Bless my soul ! I forgot all about it.

FAITH (*teasingly*). What a pity, Aunt. You said it was frightfully important, too !

PRUDENCE (*rising, with an angry glint*). I'll see to it, at once !

TILDA (*rising*). Don't bother yourself, Prudence. I'll attend to it. I know exactly what's wanted.

(TILDA *crosses and exits via door R. As she gets
off, she can be heard calling* "Cicely ! Cicely ! "
PRUDENCE *goes over L., and sits in the rocking-
chair.* FAITH *wanders over to the settee by the
window. As she does so,* BOB SLADEN *appears
outside the window. He looks into the room,
points to* PRUDENCE *and mouths the word :
"* Alone ? " FAITH *nods. He winks at her, and
disappears towards the door, back. Immediately
a sharp knock is heard.*)

PRUDENCE (*starting*). What—another one ? Who's
this ?

FAITH. I couldn't say. I didn't see anyone go
past.

PRUDENCE. If it's the dear Colonel's wife, I shall
scream ! Well, what are you waiting for ? See
who it is !

(FAITH *goes over and opens the door.*)

BOB (*hat in hand*). Hello, Faith.

FAITH (*simulating surprise*). Bob Sladen ! This
is a pleasure !

PRUDENCE. She speaks for herself, Mr. Sladen !

BOB (*entering, a shade awkwardly*). Oh—how do
you do, Ma'am ! I hadn't noticed you.

(FAITH *closes the door.*)

PRUDENCE. Very few people do seem to take any
notice of me round here. Well, young man—do
you ever do any work ?

BOB (*puzzled*). I—I beg your pardon ?

PRUDENCE. I was wondering how Applegarth
Farm could be managing without your services in
the middle of the afternoon !

BOB. Oh, there's nothing unusual in that. I've
got to pick the old man up at the station off the
four o'clock train from Town. It's a case of killing
time till then, so I thought I'd step over here and
do a bit of rehearsing.

PRUDENCE (*coldly*). With whom?

BOB. With you, Ma'am, if you wouldn't mind. Seeing that we didn't get a chance last night.

PRUDENCE (*rather flattered*). Hm! Well, you might do worse. Faith, will you please get my book? It's over in the drawer.

(FAITH *goes to the drawer and gets out the book which* TILDA *has previously used.*)

I'm afraid, Mr. Sladen, I shall have to read from the book. I haven't learnt it yet.

BOB. Neither have I—at least, not the part with you!

PRUDENCE (*taking book from* FAITH). What's this? This isn't the one! "Age Shall Not Wither."

FAITH (*taking it back*). Oh, no—that's Mother's. It's awfully good though. Have you read it, Aunt?

(FAITH *crosses to drawer, replaces book, and produces another.*)

PRUDENCE. Never even looked at it! When I get a little time, perhaps. Get me my copy, will you?

FAITH (*returning*). Here it is. "Love and a Locksmith."

PRUDENCE (*taking it*). That's better! Come and sit down, young man—here! (*She indicates chair nearest to rocking-chair.*) Now, what page is it?

BOB (*who has produced book from pocket and opened it*). Page twenty-one. Half-way down.

PRUDENCE (*turning pages*). Ah, yes. Here it is. I begin, don't I?

BOB. Yes.

PRUDENCE (*reading*). "James Fenton—I absolutely forbid you to have anything more to do with my daughter, Patricia!"

BOB. "But, Lady Fairfield——?"

PRUDENCE "Enough! You will kindly understand that this is final."

BOB. "But——?"

(*The back door opens and* NED RUDDLE *enters. He stands still for a few moments, pulling horrible faces, and holding his hand to his forehead. The others stare at him in amazement. Then he walks to the settee in front of the window, sits bolt upright, and stares straight before him, occasionally rolling his tongue around his lips, then screwing up his face into a grimace as though racked by a sudden twinge of pain.*)

PRUDENCE (*finding her tongue*). Ruddle ! What on earth's the matter with you ?

RUDDLE (*dully, eyes closed*). The sun, I reckon !

PRUDENCE. The sun ?

RUDDLE. Got me, it has—same as it got you, Saturday morning !

PRUDENCE (*angrily*). Ruddle—you've been drinking !

RUDDLE. Not me ! I wish I had. Drink never made me feel like this !

FAITH. What do you feel like, Ned ?

RUDDLE. I dunno. Same as if my back and my head were fighting and neither of 'em won't give in !

PRUDENCE. But the sun isn't strong enough !

RUDDLE. Can't be nothing else, as I can see. Besides, it weren't really strong on Saturday—and look what it did for you.

PRUDENCE (*angrily*). That was different ! Ah, well, I suppose you'd better sit there and rest quietly till it passes off.

RUDDLE (*with another grimace*). If it does !

PRUDENCE (*ignoring him and turning to* BOB). Go on, Mr. Sladen !

BOB. Where we left off ?

PRUDENCE. Yes, please.

BOB (*reading*). " But I must ask for some explanation, Lady Fairfield. I love Patrica, and she loves me ! "

PRUDENCE. " Doubtless ! Nevertheless, my de-

cision is final. There is nothing further to be said
—only one thing, perhaps ! "

BOB. "And that is ? "

(NED RUDDLE, *who has previously opened his eyes
and bestowed a prodigious wink upon* FAITH,
*suddenly pulls a horrible face, and lets out a
terrific groan.*)

RUDDLE. O—o—ouch !

PRUDENCE (*swinging sharply round*). Mercy on
us ! What ails the man ?

RUDDLE. Another spasm. It's gone now.

PRUDENCE. Then kindly keep your spasms to
yourself, and don't interfere with our rehearsing !

RUDDLE (*eyes closed*). Yes'm.

PRUDENCE (*facing round again*). Go on, Mr.
Sladen !

BOB. It's you, Ma'am !

PRUDENCE. Ah, yes ! We'll go back a little:
(*Reading.*) " Only one thing, perhaps ! "

BOB. "And that is ? "

PRUDENCE. " Good-bye ! "

RUDDLE (*in a hollow voice*). Good-bye !

PRUDENCE (*turning on him*). What are you saying " Good-bye " for ?

RUDDLE. I felt as though I were going !

BOB (*continuing*). "Lady Fairfield, I came here
to-night to ask permission to marry your daughter.
In spite of what you have said, I still intend to see
your husband to ask his consent."

PRUDENCE. "Then you may as well save your
breath ! My husband will only give you the same
answer as I, and that is——"

(*Another fearful groan from* RUDDLE.)

RUDDLE. Oo-oo-oo-ouch ! !

(*He lies back on the settee, and continues to roll
from side to side, groaning intermittently. The
others rise.*)

BOB (*crossing to* RUDDLE). There's something seriously wrong here, Miss Hannacott ! (*Shaking* RUDDLE.) Ned, old man, what's the matter ? What's wrong with you ?

RUDDLE. I dunno. Seems to have gone worse.

BOB (*L. of* RUDDLE). Your back and head, isn't it ?

RUDDLE. Aye—but I've started itching now !

PRUDENCE. Itching ?

RUDDLE. Itching all over ! (*As though he has suddenly remembered, he starts to scratch himself vigorously, jumping from place to place.*)

BOB. Itching ? (*Suddenly serious.*) Good gracious ! Surely it can't be—— ?

PRUDENCE. What ?

BOB. I was just thinking. You've heard about young Peter Yorke ?

PRUDENCE. Certainly ! That wretched Malayan complaint, isn't it ?

BOB (*seriously*). Yes. And if the symptoms are anything to go by—— (*He points to* RUDDLE, *and backs away a step.*)

PRUDENCE. Absurd !—(*But she also retreats.*) Why, Ruddle's never been anywhere near him !

BOB. I wouldn't be too sure of that ! (*To* RUDDLE.) Ned !

RUDDLE (*opening one eye*). Yes ?

BOB. Ned, do you know young Peter Yorke ?

RUDDLE (*closing the eye*). Know him ? Course I do.

BOB. Yes, but you haven't seen him lately, have you ?

RUDDLE. Seen him ? Course I have ! Been with him in the " Foresters' Arms " pretty near every night for the past two weeks.

PRUDENCE (*galvanised*). Merciful heavens !

RUDDLE. Aye—decent sort o' lad is Peter. Always was ! Gave me one of his shirts last week but one. Said he couldn't a-bear to see mine—the state it was in.

PRUDENCE (*horrified*). He did *what* ?

RUDDLE. Gave me one of his shirts. I'm wearing it now !

(PRUDENCE *hurriedly crosses to the pegs below stairs for her hat.*)

FAITH (*anxiously*). What are you going to do, Aunt ?

PRUDENCE. What am I going to do, indeed ! Do you think I'm going to stop here a second longer than I can help when there's a case of Malayan Measles running wild ?

FAITH. Then you'll be going back to Barncastle, perhaps ?

PRUDENCE. Nothing of the sort ! I'm going to find the nearest telephone and ring up for a doctor and an ambulance !

RUDDLE (*opening both eyes very wide and sitting bolt upright*). YOU'RE WHAT ?

PRUDENCE. Going to get an ambulance. You will have to be isolated, of course, and the place will have to be stoved.

RUDDLE (*horrified*). But I don't want no—— !

PRUDENCE (*at door, back*). Doctor ? Perhaps not ! But the others will !

BOB. The others ? What others ?

(TILDA *enters from door R.*)

PRUDENCE. All of you ! You'll have to be inoculated !

TILDA. Inoculated ? Who's going to be inoculated ?

PRUDENCE. You ! Faith ! (*Pointing to* BOB.) Him ! Everybody except Ruddle.

TILDA. And why not Ned ?

PRUDENCE. Because he's got it.

TILDA. Got what ?

PRUDENCE. Malayan Measles !

TILDA (*horrified*). Oh ! (*She almost collapses, and begins to weep.* FAITH *rushes over to her and helps her to the chair R. of table.*)

PRUDENCE. I shan't be long ! There's a 'phone at Marsh House just across the way.

(PRUDENCE *slams the door to behind her and exits, passing across out of sight behind the window. FAITH attends to* TILDA, *who is sobbing profusely.* RUDDLE *rises and glares at* BOB.)

BOB. Whew ! That's torn it !

RUDDLE (*going L.*). Torn it ?   So this is what comes o' your fancy idea, Bob Sladen ?

BOB (*C.—back*). Can't be helped, Ned.   Your ideas went wrong too, you know.

RUDDLE. My ideas ?   Aye—but I didn't get anybody shoved into ambulances through 'em !

BOB. Don't worry !   We'll get out of it some way.   In any case, you've nothing to bother about. They'd only shove you in hospital for a week or two if it came to the worst !

RUDDLE (*almost speechless*). ONLY ?

BOB. Anyway, you wouldn't have to be inoculated like me !

RUDDLE. Inoculated ?   You ought to be spifflicated !

TILDA (*still inconsolable*).   Inoculated ?   Oh dear !   Oh dear !

RUDDLE (*approaching her*).   Look here, Missus

TILDA. Get away !   Get away !   Don't come near me !

(RUDDLE *retreats*.)

FAITH. It's all right, Mother.   It's quite safe.

TILDA. What—with this Malayan thing ?   Never ! never !

FAITH. It is—really !   Ned hasn't got it at all.

TILDA. Hasn't got it ?

FAITH. No.   Have you, Ned ?

RUDDLE. Not a single blessed itch !

TILDA. Then—what—— ?

FAITH. It was only another of his tricks, that's all.

TILDA (*bursting out afresh*). Oh dear ! He'll be the death of me, he will ! After all that's happened, he must go and—Oh !——(*She sobs afresh.*)

BOB. Best take her upstairs, Faith, and tell her the whole story.

(FAITH *assists* TILDA *towards the stairs.*)

RUDDLE. Aye, and make sure you tell her this was one o' Bob Sladen's ideas, too !

(FAITH *and* TILDA *exit up the stairs.*)

BOB (*turning and facing* RUDDLE). Well ?
RUDDLE. Well ? I'm glad they've gone !
BOB. What for ?
RUDDLE. So I can tell you what I think about you without having to choose my words !
BOB. I shouldn't bother, Ned. Abuse won't be any help.
RUDDLE. No—but it'd be a great relief !
BOB. Listen ! We've got to get out of this mess, and there's just a chance that we can yet.
RUDDLE. How ?
BOB. Well, I've got an idea——
RUDDLE (*crossing to door, back*). Good ! Then you can do me a favour !
BOB. What's that ?
RUDDLE. You work it ! (*Making as though to exit.*) I'm going for a walk !
BOB (*fetching him back*). Come here, Ned. Don't be a fool ! It's our one chance, and we've got to take it.
RUDDLE. Well ?
BOB. You heard what she said ?
RUDDLE. What about ?
BOB. About being inoculated ? She said everybody would have to be inoculated.
RUDDLE. Except me ! I shan't forget *that* !

Bob. Well, if *everybody's* got to be inoculated, that includes *her*, doesn't it ?

Ruddle (*guardedly*). I suppose so.

Bob. Then it's up to us to scare her.

Ruddle (*sarcastically*). Aye, we haven't tried that before, have we ?

Bob. No, you don't understand. We've got to point out to her the dangers of inoculation to a woman of her age. If only we can do it well enough, she may clear out through sheer fright.

Ruddle (*dubiously*). She may !

Bob. And then we can explain it away to the doctor afterwards.

Ruddle (*hastily*). And the ambulance ! Don't forget that !

Bob. Of course not !

(Prudence *sails past the window outside, towards the door, back.*)

Bob. Look out ! Here she comes. Back on the couch !

(*He pushes* Ruddle *on to the settee.* Prudence *enters, and hangs her hat on pegs, R.*)

Prudence. Well, that's fixed. I got them both !

Bob. Both ?

Prudence. The ambulance and the doctor. The ambulance will be round any time now. The doctor may be a little longer. He said he will come over as soon as he can.

Bob (*L.C. below table*). Miss Hannacott—I've been thinking——

Prudence. Well ?

Bob. About this inoculation. We shall *all* have to be inoculated, I suppose ?

Prudence. Undoubtedly !

Bob. I—er—I don't want to influence you in any way, but do you think it's altogether safe ?

Prudence. What ?

Bob. Inoculation. I've read quite a lot about it. It seems that in the case of elderly people—

women mostly— it produces rather terrible results.

PRUDENCE. Really? I wasn't aware of it.

BOB. Yes. In fact in many instances—women of about your own age, Miss Hannacott, it has been proved to have done more harm than good.

PRUDENCE. And what is this leading to?

BOB. I was only thinking that if I were you, I should be very chary of——

PRUDENCE. I understand. It's very kind of you, Mr. Sladen, to take such an interest in me. However, you can set your mind completely at rest. I have no intention of being inoculated!

BOB (*aghast*). But you said we should *all* ——?

PRUDENCE. Exactly! But I did not include myself. I am *not* going to be inoculated!

BOB. But if you don't, you can't possibly stop here with—this! (*Pointing to* RUDDLE.)

PRUDENCE. Can't I? (*Crossing to door L.*) Oh, yes, I can! You see, I was inoculated before I went on a cruise last year. Inoculated against everything!

(*With a triumphant smile,* PRUDENCE *exits through door, L. As the door bangs,* RUDDLE *jumps up and rushes for the door, back.*)

BOB. Here, Ned! Where are you going?

(SAMUEL MEACOCK *passes across behind window.*)

RUDDLE. The pig-styes!

BOB. What for?

RUDDLE. To get out o' the road o' that ambulance!

(RUDDLE *flings open the door and rushes out, nearly bowling over* MEACOCK, *who is just about to enter. However, he stays for no apology, but dashes blindly off, R.* BOB *follows after him to the door.*)

BOB. Ned! Come back! Come back! (*He brushes past* MEACOCK.) Oh, how do you do, Mr. Meacock!

MEACOCK (*big, bluff and hearty*).   Hallo, Bob !
What's up with Ned ?

BOB. Nothing much. Sorry I can't stay !

MEACOCK. Anybody at home ? (*Peering in.*)

BOB. There'll be someone shortly. Excuse me !
(*He rushes off after* RUDDLE.)

MEACOCK (*shrugging his shoulders*). H'm !

(MEACOCK *enters and closes the door behind him.
He holds his bowler hat across his chest and
stares around. A moment later, the door L.
opens, and* PRUDENCE *enters. She looks across
at the settee and gasps.*)

PRUDENCE. Good heavens ! Where's Ruddle ?

MEACOCK. Just gone out, Ma'am !

PRUDENCE. The fool ! Still, he won't have much
longer to run around. (*Realising* MEACOCK *is a
stranger.*)   And you, sir—what might be your
business ?

MEACOCK. Excuse me, Ma'am. Miss Hannacott,
I believe ?

PRUDENCE. I am. And you ?

MEACOCK. Meacock's the name, Ma'am. Samuel
Meacock ! You know about me ?

PRUDENCE. Ah, yes ! Well, I'm afraid, Mr.
Meacock, that my sister——

MEACOCK. Oh, don't bother about her. It's you
I want. Come specially to get it over in private.

PRUDENCE. Indeed ?

MEACOCK. Yes. Well—there's nothing like getting down to it right away. Ready, Ma'am ?

PRUDENCE (*at a loss*). Yes, I—I suppose so.

MEACOCK. Then here goes ! (*He deposits his
bowler hat on the dresser, then throws out his chest,
clears his throat, and adopts a masterful attitude.*)
" Sit down ! "

PRUDENCE. I—I beg your pardon !

MEACOCK (*very forceful*). " Sit down ! "

PRUDENCE (*each reply a shade more nervous from
this time on*). Really—I——

MEACOCK. That's not the answer ! "Sit down !"

PRUDENCE. W-where ?

MEACOCK. "There ! " (*He indicates chair R. of table. She sits.*) " Prudence—I may call you Prudence, I suppose ? "

PRUDENCE. H-how dare you !

MEACOCK. That's wrong ! You say : " Certainly, if you wish."

PRUDENCE. I—I—don't !

MEACOCK. Yes, you do ! Go on—say it !

PRUDENCE. C-certainly, if you wish.

MEACOCK (*kneeling beside her*). " Prudence— ever since you came to this place I have worshipped you from afar. You have inspired me with the heavenly fire. Yet this is the first time I have dared approach you."

PRUDENCE. But—I—I——

MEACOCK. Be quiet ! I haven't finished. " Maybe you look upon me as a stranger—but I am no stranger. Everywhere you have been these last few weeks, I have followed you ! "

PRUDENCE. E-everywhere ?

MEACOCK. Good ! That's right. " Everywhere ! When you go to bed, I stand outside and look for your beloved shadow on the blind."

PRUDENCE (*outraged*). Really—I—I—— !

MEACOCK. Wait for it ! I haven't half-finished yet ! " Prudence—neither of us is in the first flush of youth—but such love as theirs is not for us. Theirs is here to-day and gone to-morrow. But the slow burning passion of middle-age is lasting— consuming ! "

PRUDENCE. H-have you q-quite finished ?

MEACOCK. No, there's a lot more yet ! " Prudence—I want you to make a great decision. I love you—long for you—hunger for you ! I must have an answer to-night ! You shall not escape me, even though you say ' No.' For I shall follow you everywhere—haunt you—until I have made you mine ! "

PRUDENCE. A-are you suggesting m-marriage?

MEACOCK. You should say: " Do you wish to marry me? ". Go on—say it!

PRUDENCE. D-do you wish to marry me?

MEACOCK. " Marriage? Pah! What is marriage? No, Prudence—something more wonderful—more pulsating—more vital! "

PRUDENCE. WHAT?

MEACOCK. Don't interrupt! I'll tell you when! " We can be ideally happy; and when we tire— why, then—we can go our separate ways, and end as perfectly as we began. Prudence—you cannot refuse me—you shall not refuse me! For if you do—I shall still have you—for by Heaven, I shall carry you away by force."

PRUDENCE (*screaming and breaking out into hysterics*). Help! Help! HELP!

(*She continues to scream, stamping her feet on the ground, and beating her fists on her knees. MEACOCK rises astounded. He tries to quieten her, but that only increases her vocal efforts. TILDA and FAITH enter from the stairs, CICELY from the door R.; BOB and RUDDLE from door back. RUDDLE carries a pail of water. They all group round most concernedly. RUDDLE makes as though to dash the bucket of water over her. Realising this, she stops screaming, jumps up, runs over to the pegs below stairs and starts pulling on her hat. She is almost choking with indignation. The rest stare in wonder.*)

TILDA. Prudence! Where are you going?

PRUDENCE. Going? Away from here for ever!

RUDDLE (*almost dropping his bucket*). WHAT?

PRUDENCE. Tilda Hannacott, you may run your farm as you please—ruin it too, if you like! As for me, I'll never set foot in your house again!

TILDA. But, Prudence——?

PRUDENCE. Never again! I'm going back to

Barncastle—back to sane people !   (*To* MEACOCK.)
And as for you, vile monster, if ever you come
near, or attempt to lure me into your evil clutches
again, I'll have the Police on you, that I will !
Praise heaven, I found you out in time, that I may
leave this den of iniquity unsullied and unashamed !
Good-bye. (*She stalks towards the back door.*)

TILDA. But Prudence—your things ?

PRUDENCE. You can send them after me—Good-
bye !

(*As she turns to go,* MRS. MIDDLETON-JONES *and* MISS
LOVEDAY *appear in the doorway.*)

MIDDLETON-JONES. Ah, dear Miss Hannacott !
I've come to apologise for——

PRUDENCE. Get out of my way—you old `hay-
bags !

(*They part in astonishment. She sails between
them, out of the door and away past the window.* LOVEDAY *and* MIDDLETON-JONES *turn and
stare after her. The door remains ajar.*)

MIDDLETON-JONES (*turning to front again*). Hay-
bags ? Really !

FAITH. Mr. Meacock. What happened ?

MEACOCK. Blest if I know !   I was rehearsing
my part with her, that's all. (*Producing book from
pocket.*) Here it is, see—"Age Shall Not Wither "
—Cast—Prudence Berryman — Miss Hannacott—
that's her !

TILDA. But that's my part !

MEACOCK. What !

LOVEDAY. Let me see.   (*She takes the book.*)
Dear me ! It's my fault, I'm afraid. I should have
put " Mrs." and I went and put " Miss." Stupid of
me, wasn't it ?

RUDDLE. Not a bit !

LOVEDAY. Anyhow, I've remembered now what
it was I came to tell you. It was about Mr.
Meacock.

TILDA. Mr. Meacock?

LOVEDAY. Yes, about him coming to rehearse with you this afternoon.   But it's too late now, isn't it?

RUDDLE. It is—by Gad, it is!

BOB. Here, Ned! (*Offering note.*) Your pound —you've earned it.

RUDDLE. Wait a minute! (*Taking note, and putting it into MEACOCK's hand.*) Here, Sammy, my lad—it's yours!

MEACOCK. What for?

RUDDLE. You've earned it! (*Taking him by the arm.*) Come on!

MEACOCK. Where are we going?

RUDDLE. Back to the "Foresters' Arms." You've won a pound, and I'm going to help you spend it. Come on!

(*He drags MEACOCK off, and they exit through the back door, leaving it still ajar, and off towards the R.—N.B.—They do not pass the window.*)

MIDDLETON-JONES. My dear Mrs. Hannacott, I'm afraid I don't quite understand!

FAITH. It's only this, Mrs. Middleton-Jones— you'll have to find a new Lady Fairfield—that's all.

MIDDLETON-JONES. But why?

FAITH. Aunt Prudence has gone to live at Barncastle—for her health.

MIDDLETON-JONES. Oh.

(*An ambulance-bell is heard ringing outside.*)

FAITH. And there's another piece of news, too. Bob Sladen and I are going to be married. Aren't we, Mother?

TILDA. Yes, dear. I suppose so.

MIDDLETON-JONES. Congratulations, dear!

LOVEDAY. And mine, too! How perfectly—perfectly splendid!

CICELY. Fa-ancy tha-at!

(They are administering their congratulations to
Bob *and* Faith, *when there is a terrible shouting
from outside, unmistakably the voice of* Ruddle.
The ambulance-bell rings again.)

Ruddle *(off)*. Help ! Help ! Missus ! Bob
Sladen ! Don't let them take me ! Here, stop it,
I tell you ! Help ! Help !

(They all turn in astonishment. Suddenly Ned
Ruddle *rushes through the door R., closely
followed by a couple of supers in white coats
who are vainly endeavouring to get hold of him.
He circles right round the room, still shouting
and dodging the assembled company. When he
comes round to the door in the back wall, he
disappears through it, passing* Meacock, *who
has appeared there.* Meacock *tries to bar the
supers' exit, while* Ruddle *outside the window
shakes his fist at* Bob *and* Faith. *After a moment
or two,* Meacock *is swept aside and* Ruddle
*disappears from the window chased by the
supers.* Bob *and* Faith *cross to the door, laughing and waving their hands. The ambulance-
bell continues to ring violently, as—*

the CURTAIN *slowly falls.*

PRODUCTION NOTES BY THE AUTHOR.

May I begin by stressing that "The Camel's Back" is a comedy, and not farce. The interest of the play, from start to finish, is based upon the conflict between Prudence and the rest of the Hannacott household. Ned Ruddle bears the brunt of the attack, and the definite contrast between these two strong characters must be clearly brought out : Prudence—cold and calculating, with her biting remarks ; and Ruddle, with the sly dig and impassive countenance.

It need not be emphasised that these parts should not be over-acted, as much of the humour would be lost by forcing. For heaven's sake do not make Ruddle a farcical character !

Tilda is completely under the thumb ; but Faith is torn between loyalty to her Mother and good-natured resentment of her Aunt's domination.

Bob Sladen is not a yokel by any means, nor yet a matinee idol—a straight-forward young man, passive in the anti-Prudence campaign at first, but assuming more control in the last desperate effort— the Malayan Measles episode in Act III.

There should be a sharp contrast between the fussy Miss Loveday and the prim and proper Mrs. Middleton-Jones. Loveday's chatty out-pouring and well-meant enthusiasm will show up all the better against the more formal attitude of Middleton-Jones.

Cicely is a real country type—slow on the uptake, and completely overawed by Prudence, and the threats of Ruddle in Act III.

Meacock, from the moment he enters in Act III, must entirely dominate the scene. He is a man with no small regard for his own abilities, and intends to display how good an actor he is. His delivery of the lines, which he fondly imagines himself to be rehearsing, must be exaggerated and gain in pace and intensity in proportion to the collapse of Prudence's resistance. His last two speeches prior to the climax must work up to a top note of histrionic effort. This will serve to heighten his subsequent bewilderment.

Now for the setting. A box-set would undoubtedly be more effective, but the play can be presented in curtains with practicable flats for doors and window. The door on the back wall should open inwards—the other two, right and left, off-stage. Have a light-blue cloth behind the window and light it from below as strongly as possible, avoiding shadows.

The furniture may be a judicious blend of ancient and modern—the Welsh dresser, grandfather clock, warming-pan, etc., in sharp contrast to the parlour grate and upholstered settee beneath the window. Let the stage lighting be as bright as possible for Acts I and III. An overhead baby-spot trained on the Welsh dresser, set out with shining pewter and willow-pattern crockery, would be most effective. For Act II, the lighting should be more subdued to conform with the table oil-lamp. The window curtains and curtains across the stair-opening should be drawn, and the back-cloth lighting must be dispensed with during this scene.

The falling picture in Act II calls for a little ingenuity. A hole bored through the framework of the flat and a rod pushed through from the back and projecting an inch or so in front will serve to support the picture. This can be withdrawn from behind at the appropriate moment and the picture will crash down most effectively. But, please, Mr: Stage-Manager, do make sure that it is firm ! If it should happen to come down in the wrong place I can well visualise the complete collapse of the players and your reputation !

You will find sufficient notes in the play with regard to movements and positions, but do not follow these blindly as they are only suggestions. After all, I don't know your stage, and you don't have to work on mine.

I would like, however, to warn you against one thing. Do not let your players imagine that the front edge of the table represents the footlights. There is a danger of allowing too much action to take place *behind* that table, so do not be afraid to bring your characters well down whenever possible.

Finally, I must urge the importance of *speed* and *attack*. The play must not be allowed to drag at any point, and it should gather in pace to the last Act.

The "rehearsal" parts need careful handling. For example Bob and Faith in Act I must make it obvious that they are reading their script for the first time. In the early part of Act II a subtle change in attack will suggest that they are more conversant with the same passage.

Again, the general "rehearsal" in Act II should be somewhat exaggerated to contrast with the ordinary atmosphere of the farm-house.

It is up to Prudence and Miss Loveday to force the pace along whenever they appear ; and Ruddle, Bob and Faith must do likewise whenever plots are a-brewing or the action is working up to a climax.

HAND PROPERTIES.
ACT I.
Pair of step-ladders.

Hammer	RUDDLE
Two pot eggs	RUDDLE
Handkerchief	TILDA
Two script copies	BOB
Four or five script copies	LOVEDAY
Pound note	BOB
Glass flask containing water	RUDDLE
Empty flask (*same one*)	CICELY
Fairly large tea-pot	LOVEDAY

ACT II.

Copy of script	FAITH
Tray, with plates, butter, cheese, table-cloth, biscuits	CICELY
Copy of script	BOB
Copy of script	RUDDLE
Copy of script	LOVEDAY
Two half-crowns	LOVEDAY
Copy of script	MIDDLETON-JONES
Ten shilling note	MIDDLETON-JONES
Copy of script	PRUDENCE
Tray with five glasses and jug of milk	CICELY
Long nightgown	RUDDLE
Jug from wash hand-basin	RUDDLE
Knife	RUDDLE

ACT III.

Tray for	CICELY
Tray containing used crockery	FAITH
Half-crown	CICELY
Copy of script	TILDA
Copy of script	BOB
One script copy in dresser drawer (*Must be there at beginning of Act.*)	
Script copy	MEACOCK
Bucket of water	RUDDLE
Pound note	BOB
Ambulance-bell	Off-stage

FURNITURE PLOT, ETC.

Dresser. Settee.
Grandfather clock.
Table.
Four chairs (One a Rocking Chair).
One arm-chair.
Pewter and Willow-pattern crockery for dresser.
Warming-pan.
Bright chintz curtains for window.
Heavier dark curtain for stair-opening.
Small picture (gilt frame) above stairs.
Larger portrait of "the dear-departed Master"
    above fireplace.

ACT 1.

Table set. Remains of breakfast.
Tray on dresser.
Step-ladders on stage.

ACT II.

Oil lamp burning on table.
Newspaper placed on table.
Curtains drawn (window and stairs).

ACT III.

As Act I for setting, except that small picture has
    disappeared and arm-chair is back again at L.
Few pots and cloth on table.
Curtain open as in Act I.
One script copy planted in dresser drawer for
    PRUDENCE.

110

Lightning Source UK Ltd.
Milton Keynes UK
UKOW06f0000130516

274163UK00001B/71/P